Eliminating the Greener Grass Trap

Quitting the Habit of Comparisons

By

Linda Rose Killian

Acknowledgments

This book has been an on-going process for several years and has been in my thoughts, and incorporated into some of my writings in my Devotional Blog: "Devotional Fuel Pulls To Reboot Your Mind—Redirecting our thoughts to God's truths and promises." I want to thank my husband, Steve, for continuing to encourage me to get this book completed—to get it done and for believing in me as a writer. I need to thank many that have given me feedback on this project, such as Erika Seibert, and Kathlee Coleman, in helping me in preparing for the final revised manuscript before turning it into being a completed book at last, in the hands of John Manning, Book Designer Pro.

Contents

Introduction

One day a fellow businessman, who was a customer in my sales job, and a friend, said to me, "Linda, my lawn is not any greener. Let me tell you what I am dealing with today: I have four pallets of shampoo with the fragrance that my customer chose, and now he does not like it! What am I going to do with four pallets of rejected bottles of shampoo?" Then he went on to say: "What you do for others lasts forever. This stuff doesn't." Those three sentences stuck in my mind for days. What I am struggling with today will not matter a month from now or a year from now, and I may not even remember it happening. What I or what we do for God will count for all eternity and not just for today. When I compare my current circumstances and want to trade them with anyone else, I find in the end that they have their struggles in life too. They just might be afraid to share the particular struggle they are experiencing.

The old proverb "the grass is always greener on the other side of the fence" came from people viewing other people's lives or situations always better than their own even if it is not the case. When we look at other people's circumstances, it often seems like their life is perfect. It usually deals with a state of happiness, and contentment is not in the equation. It is that inner yearning and longing due to dissatisfaction of thinking that someone else appears to have a carefree life filled with more material possessions than you happen to have.

I look at others and often feel inferior and forget they are going through hard times as well. They may be hiding it and not tell me about it, or I may not even be able to see their "it." My friend's metaphor that his lawn was not any greener than mine spoke volumes to me. God will take him down a different path than God will take me to strengthen, fortify, and mold us to become more like Christ. The road and order of Romans 8:28, "working everything out for my good," runs through a different route for me than anyone else, and often I can't see the right GPS route to get to God's intended final destination. But I confess, I often look at others and envy something about their life's situation over mine. Do you do that too? That is when inferiority, insecurity, and feeling insignificant always take residence.

This common problem of women comparing ourselves to other women is the subject of this book and what the result will always be when we do that. I admit I have struggled with this predicament most of my life. Why do we so often do this? When you have a "bad hair day," doesn't it sometimes ruin your whole day? You may think that everyone is staring at that one spot that did not turn out right in the back of your head, or on top or the side. It serves in your mind as a visual picture of one of your flaws. In reality, no one else views that place on your head as a flaw at all. It merely hinges on your perspective.

We women so often think somebody else has it better than we do. That old saying—"The grass is greener on the other side of the fence" is called "looking through rose-colored glasses." This saying is said to have come from looking at a neighbor's lawn and seeing it greener, healthier, better looking than our own when in reality we are ignoring anything negative about it and downplaying anything positive about our own. There are weeds there; you just cannot see them hidden within the green grass at first glance.

Does this resonate with you at all? I fall into this temptation of wrong thinking too often and feel I am a failure. But there is a "but!" Yes, but God never requires us to be perfect and knows we cannot be perfect. He is our hope! God calls us His "beloved." We are adored, cherished, treasured, prized, esteemed, and dearly loved. 1 John 3:1-2 tells us: "See what kind of love the Father has given to us that we should be called children of God; and so we are. The reason why the world does not know us is that it did not know him. Beloved, we are God's children now, and what we will be has not yet appeared; but we know that when he appears we shall be like him, because we shall see him as he is." That day is becoming closer each day!

Is my grass any greener than yours? Is your lawn any greener than mine? No, is the answer to both questions. Explore life as God intends for you and fully realize that we are encircled by God's love all day long. With His love, He will calm all our fears of insecurity. He has said in 1 John 3:2b that when Christ returns for us, "we shall be like him, because we shall see him as he is." I so look forward to that day as it says in Revelation 21:4: "He shall wipe away every tear from their eyes, and death shall be no more, neither shall there be mourning, nor crying, nor pain anymore, for the former things have passed away." When Christ returns for us to take us to our eternal home in Heaven, we will have heavenly bodies. We will have no more reason to compare ourselves to anyone else because we will be like our Savior. But for now, we live on this earth day by day. So, sister, my grass is not greener than yours. Your lawn is not greener than mine. Let us fight together this battle of comparing ourselves to each other and feeling less than good enough.

Come with me on a journey in exploring this ageless dilemma and eliminate the greener grass trap. Let us explore quitting the habit of comparisons that will only lead to insecurities once and for all.

All scripture references are taken primarily from the ESV unless stated otherwise.

1

The Old Temptation Of Envy

God is our shepherd and overseer, as Peter said in 1 Peter 2:25, "For you were straying like sheep, but have now returned to the Shepherd and Overseer of your souls." Think about those last six words in this verse—"Shepherd and Overseer of your souls." God patiently guides us in what His purpose for us is in our life to bring glory to our Lord and Savior. He has given each of us something to do that shows who God is.

Psalm 28:7 declares, "The Lord is my strength and my shield . . ." Various shields protect us from harm. God told Abraham in Genesis 15:1, "Fear not, Abram, I am your shield." Our faith in God shepherding and overseeing us is our shield of protection in life, but why do we so often compare our experience with others that *appear* to be carefree and wonder if we are the only ones carrying heavy burdens? If the Bible tells us God is our shepherd, overseer, and our shield of protection, why do we feel lacking in comparison to someone else's life?

Proverbs 14:30 states, "A tranquil heart gives life to the flesh, but envy makes the bones rot."

Have you shielded your life from the stumbling block and the secret sin of "envy?" I don't think envy is talked much about it being a sin in our Christian circles in comparison to the time spent focusing on other sins. Instead, we harp against adultery, lying, hate, immorality, pornography, divorce, gluttony, and lack of self-control, but have we examined our heart against the sin of envy?

According to dictionary.com, the word "envy" used as a noun means: "A feeling of discontentment or resentful longing, aroused by someone else's possessions, qualities, or luck." When used as a verb, it said it means: "A desire to have a quality, possession, or other desirable attribute belonging to someone else." Synonyms are jealousy and covetousness. The words envy and jealousy are very close in meaning.

I can remember three seemingly prominent women that I at one time envied and felt that they all had more than I did in life. They had larger homes than I did. Each house was beautifully decorated with just the right accent pieces. We had just moved from the mid-west to California, so our real estate situation was starting over from scratch, and there was an immense economic gap geographically. There is a massive difference in real estate pricing and square footage between the mid-west and California. California homes cost about double and were half the size in comparison. One woman, who had previously lived in our same town in the mid-west had explained to me that in California housing, "Your patio is another room to your house." It made sense when I changed my frame of reference to that concept.

These women seemed to have it all—beautiful and spacious homes. I remember one woman had decorative dark green dinner plates sitting out on their kitchen table with the appropriate placemat underneath each setting. This place setting was set out for appearance's sake only. I had never seen that before. Then they each had husbands that had secure jobs and thrived within their employment. My situation seemed lacking in comparison.

However, several years later, two out of the three couples had severe health trials in life. One of the three women's husband was taken home to glory from his unexpected battle with cancer, and the woman herself had a bout with cancer but wholly recovered. Another woman also experienced cancer, and her husband did as well. The one couple thankfully have both recovered from their respective cancer diseases. The third woman later had challenging troubles in her life as well. So there was a portion of each of these women I had envied that experienced hardship later in life. Their grass was not greener after all. I coveted these women's material possessions and economic status. Their homes seemed more prominent and more beautiful than mine. Their husbands appeared to be happier in their jobs, at the time, than mine back then. But as I look back now, they each went through crisis circumstances later in life. Cancer attacked four out of the six people. Three recovered and survived; the one man did not.

God gives us His commandment, which is part of the Ten Commandments, back in Exodus 20:17: "You shall not covet (envy) your neighbor's house, you shall not covet your neighbor's wife, or his male servant, or his female servant, or his ox, or his donkey, or anything that is your neighbor's." There were four commandments before this one. They focused on actions or words spoken. However, the tenth commandment, verse 17, focuses on a warning of the heart—coveting anything that is your neighbors. When a person wants or envies, he allows the desire for the object to govern one's relationship with another person. Bitterness often is the motivation behind murders, stealing, or lying to obtain the desired item. Coveting or envy obstructs complete faith and trust in God to provide all things. Obedience in the LORD requires full acceptance in what God has given one to use and enjoy in his or her own life.

Paul declares in Ephesians 5:5 that wanting what others have in comparison to your own is idolatry. Covetousness looks upon material possessions with an unthankful heart for what God has provided in one's own life. We are telling God that He has not done a good enough job when we look with wistful intent at what others have and have a resentful longing that we do not have it too. Instead, we need to focus on thankfulness and praising God for all of the mercy and grace He has freely given to each one of us. When you write out a list of what God has done in your life, instead of what you have done in your life, your focus turns from inward to upward. Practice this regularly and watch how your attitude changes.

Paul firmly stated in Colossians 3:5: "Put to death therefore what is earthly in you: sexual immorality, impurity, passion, evil desire, and covetousness, which is idolatry." Paul called out the sin of envy—covetousness. Greed will steal our affection away from God. Worshiping and praising God, on the other hand, destroys envying others and squelches materialism.

Envying others will blind us to our sins. It causes our thoughts, desires, and energies to be placed on the wrong focus of material things that do not have lasting value. It is one of Satan's strategies that will cause our peace and joy and contentment to be depleted so that we will be less effective in God's purpose for our life. The sin of envy destroys our relationship with our creator and others. Instead, we need to reroute our thoughts back to seeking after God and in putting Him first in our life.

A dear friend of mine posted on Facebook a beautiful quote from Wisdom Hunters written by Boyd Bailey: "Envy harbored in a heart can easily grow into resentful outcomes that fuel anger and steal joy. However, when you release your envy by being grateful for God's blessings and refuse to compare your life to another's, you are free to enjoy contented living."

King Solomon, who is attributed traditionally as the author of Ecclesiastes, was a very wealthy and blessed king in Jerusalem. He reigned in one of the most prosperous periods of Israel's history. The Bible states that God gave Solomon wisdom, as is stated in Ecclesiastes 1:16: "I said in my heart, "I have acquired great wisdom, surpassing all who were over Jerusalem before me, and my heart has had great experience of wisdom and knowledge." However, Solomon learned a great lesson in life. He asks the question in Ecclesiastes 1:2b-3, "Vanity of vanities! All is vanity. What does man gain by all the toil at which he toils under the sun?" Solomon learned that pleasures and achievements are fleeting. Wealth and honor are not permanent, and hardship and sacrifice do not always guarantee an abundant bank account or savings account.

Money can be lost in a dangerous venture as Solomon states in Ecclesiastes 6:14, "And those riches were lost in a bad venture." Oh, how we learn profound lessons from our mistakes with money, rather than our successes! Therefore, the experience

Solomon believes to be learned is that we are to enjoy a good day's work during our lifetime. Verses 19-20 states, "Everyone also to whom God has given wealth and possessions and power to enjoy them, and to accept his lot and riches in his toil— this is the gift of God. For he will not much remember the days of his life because God keeps him occupied with joy in his heart."

The secret of not allowing envy to reign in our hearts is to be filled with the joy that can only be obtained by walking obediently, one day at a time with the Lord Jesus Christ. When I see a sunset, that is a sign to me that the daylight is about finished for that day. I need to accept each day as a gift from God in what time God has given me to live for Him since He knows the number of days I have to live on this earth. God's grace and mercy, given to me abundantly, are gifts to cling to one day at a time.

Jesus is my overseer. He is my shepherd. He is my strength and my shield and fills my heart with overflowing joy. Happiness is not always the result. But joy, filling my heart by the Holy Spirit, is like an overflowing bubbly fountain, which brings permanent and lasting satisfaction. God rescues His children due to His eternal love and puts His love into action. So how can I feel lacking in His purpose for me on this earth? Achievements and positions in life are fleeting. My successes are not my identity. God's promises for my life are full of blessings and goodness.

Psalm 23:1: "The LORD is my shepherd; I shall not want." The NIV states it this way: "The LORD is my shepherd. I lack nothing." Now repeat after me, "I lack nothing!"

⸭ Questions ⸭

1. What are you lacking (what don't you have) that would make you more content?

2. Do you feel fulfilled in life? Why or why not?

3. Who have you envied, and why?

2

Feel Inadequate? Don't Quit

"Now the word of the LORD came to Jonah the son of Amittai, saying "Arise, go to Nineveh, that great city, and call out against it, for their evil has come up before me." But Jonah rose to flee to Tarshish from the presence of the LORD. He went down to Joppa and found a ship going to Tarshish. So he paid the fare and went on board, to go with them to Tarshish, away from the presence of the LORD."
Jonah 1:1-3

Do you remember the story of Jonah? God instructed Jonah to go to Nineveh. The Bible says that Nineveh was a great city, and it was a large city. It was a mighty city that exerted significant influence over the Middle East until her destruction by Nebuchadnezzar in 612 B.C. It was possibly the largest city in the world at that time. Tarshish was known for its sizeable wealth. It is said that their population could have approached 600,000. Today that would be equal to the size of Milwaukee, Wisconsin. Nineveh was the center of worship of idols by the name of Assur and Ishtar. But

Jonah fled instead to "Tarshish, from the presence of the LORD." Yet the town of Nineveh is where God commanded Jonah to go to preach God's message and rebuke the reluctance of Jews to bring Gentiles to the true God.

Jonah is the only recorded instance of a prophet refusing God's commission. He felt *inadequate* and was no doubt fearful in his feelings of inferiority in accomplishing the assignment God had given him to do, so he ran the opposite direction, seeking greener pastures.

Has God given you a job to do? Do you feel inadequate and inferior because you are comparing yourself to someone else that you think can or could do it better than yourself? Are you feeling discouraged in your abilities and just don't feel you are good enough? Don't quit! Jonah tried to quit and look at what happened to him? Don't go down that path. Satan is not going to let you or I succeed if he can. That is the point. That is just the time to focus on God's strength and the fact that He is the *overseer* of your soul.

Quitting is easy. But plowing through perseverance and developing endurance takes work. Remembering past answers to prayers gives us the encouragement of God's power in our lives. I so often forget that and have to take out a box that I have a gift tag on that says: "To Linda and Family. From: God." When I read over the many answers to prayers that I have written down on cards and placed inside this gift box, they remind me that yes, nothing is too hard for God and that God is powerful and works in ways we cannot even see. As my Grandma Helmers always said, "This too shall pass."

Jonah got it in the end and became obedient after living in the belly of that whale for three days and three nights. Look at what Jonah ends up declaring in Jonah 2:7-10: "When my life was fainting away, I remembered the LORD, and my prayer came to you, into your holy temple. Those who pay regard to vain idols forsake their hope of steadfast love. But I with the voice of thanksgiving will sacrifice to you; what I have vowed I will pay. Salvation belongs to the LORD! And the LORD spoke to the fish, and it vomited Jonah upon the dry land."

Yes, salvation belongs to the LORD. God demands our obedience. Don't be a quitter. We must trust and place our faith and hope in God, as Jonah eventually learned to do.

Jonah remembered the LORD, but he had to hit rock bottom before he remembered to look up to God in obedience. He mentions, "vain idols." So often, when we compare what we have or don't have, our possessions or lot in life with another woman that has more than we do, our focus is on "vain idols." Material possession(s) is someone else's treasures. It may be someone else's bigger house, or a bigger kitchen, or a lavish backyard with a beautiful swimming pool, a dining room light fixture, a more massive diamond ring, or a Tesla, or some other make of car, or better or cuter clothes. We all have our idols of desires of things that someone else has, but we don't have. It is an old on-going comparison game, those idols of the heart that we hold onto, and that turns it back on God's sovereignty.

I live in a small to moderate size California house. We have 1560 square feet to our home. When we remodeled our kitchen, we knocked out two walls that ultimately opened up the kitchen into the dining room and living room areas. It gave it an open feeling we didn't have before. I still feel our house is small. But I prayed that when we finished this remodeling project, that we would have rich fellowship in this new area—that someone would come to know the Lord in our new kitchen and dining area. I asked God that hearts would be blessed and drawn to Christ within this new room. We love to cook and have friends sit at our island and talk about answers to prayer as we are finishing the meal preparations. This setting creates intimacy, bonding, and warm fellowship. The size of the space does not limit the potential of developing deeper friendships. I still wish our house was more substantial in size, but the square footage of our home is what God has given us, and we want to use it to bless others.

I finally came to realize that the size of my kitchen or house does not give its meaning or make up its importance. The size of one's home does not make their grass any greener than others. What counts is sharing what is in your heart—your love, your concerns, your passion for encouraging other people in your home that God has given you. It all belongs to Him, and He expects us to be good stewards graciously and share it with others.

Write out a list on a piece of paper on everything you do at your job (if you are working). Next, write everything down you have done in your home for the day. Look at both lists. It takes completing accomplishments in the process of finishing each task, and you did it! Now compare your current role in life and responsibilities to that of a year ago. Quite a difference, right? Look how far God has brought you in the process! It is like starting a new exercise program. At first, you think you will never be able to do all of the paces or sets of the schedule. But then you work at it every day, and it suddenly becomes more comfortable, and your lungs don't get out of breath because you didn't give up and quit. God will open doors for you beyond your imagination if you seek Him first. You are not inadequate. God gave you talents, and gifts only meant for you to accomplish great things for Him and His glory.

Do you feel like you have lost your confidence when comparing yourself to someone else you much admire? Brokenness, discouragement, and despair flood in its place. I have been there many times. We have to recognize our weaknesses, shortcomings, and put on humility. Then cast all your anxiety upon the Lord (1 Peter 5:7), and praise God He is with you, and He is able to use you despite your flaws. Ask Him to make you of benefit and wait and watch for blessings you hadn't expected.

My grass is not any greener than yours. I feel inadequate in areas that you no doubt are better equipped than I am, and that is what makes up a team of unified girlfriends. Don't allow Satan to tempt you with doubts and discouragement. That is the danger zone you want to stop yourself from falling into that trap. Don't give up and don't quit because God is walking right beside you. You are making progress.

Questions

1. What new accomplishment have you been able to do for the first time recently?

2. Look up Exodus 3:11-12. What was Moses afraid of? What was God's response to Moses? How did God not answer Moses's question (note God's words to Moses), and what did He say instead?

3. How can you serve God right where you are?

3

God Formed Me

"For you formed my inward parts; you knitted me together in my mother's womb. I praise you, for I am fearfully and wonderfully made. Wonderful are your works; my soul knows it very well."

Psalm 139:13-14

In looking at various fashion magazines our culture popularizes, don't we women often wish we looked like that model on the cover of that magazine? How often I feel I am not pretty enough, smart enough, or witty enough. I compare myself to other women that appear to be more successful and have so many more friends than I do. If someone doesn't say hi to me in a group setting, I am afraid they must be upset with me for some reason or don't like me. Do you do that too? What about struggling to feel like you belong at work, or church, or within your own family?

I compare myself to other writers and women speakers and wish I sounded like them. I just counted the use of the word "I" seven times in only four sentences. That is the real problem—dwelling too much on myself rather than others.

God made Jonah unique for the task He planned for only Jonah to do. Likewise, God has done the same for each one of us. God has made each one of us unique in giving us talents and spiritual gifts that He intended for each one of us to do. God has given you something unique, presented to you by the Spirit of God, by His sovereign design and proportion.

Remember when you used to cut out snowflakes in grade school and taped them on the windows? Photographers have found great stunning scientific variety in shooting snowflakes. They have to capture each snowflake quickly before they melt. Each snowflake has its crystal shape. Did you know that snowflakes always have six sides, and no two are the same? They look like crystals falling from the sky. When it snows, catching a glimpse of snowflakes is a beautiful sight that God created. If they were all the same, they wouldn't capture the beauty of each ice crystal shaped into each unique captured image.

When I was a young girl, I envied other girls and women that had fuller sized legs than mine. You may find this surprising. I felt my skinny legs were a curse. I can remember sitting in the waiting room of my small town's hospital while my parents were visiting a member of our church. I sat there and stared at every woman's legs that walked passed. I critiqued and chose which ones I wish I had instead. I even used to ride my bicycle every day because I had read that it would increase the size of the muscles in my legs. Guess what. It didn't work. As my mother would try to make me feel better about my skinny legs, she would try to convince me that girls with fuller legs were jealous of my slender legs and wished they had mine. I didn't believe her.

My skinny legs come from my Grandma Helmers, which was my mother's mom. Grandma Helmers had very long and slender legs, and my body frame was inherited actually from her. Long skinny legs and being short-waisted was my inherited body frame from Grandma Helmers. I think each one of us women has something about our body shape that we wish we could change. But as a teenager, that didn't console me at the time. Dissatisfaction inwardly took over.

God has said He made me. He is the almighty creator of all human life and all of creation. Why do we women have such a hard time accepting our body frame that cannot be changed and that He created? It comes down to what my mother would say to me so often during those insecure teenage girl days, "Get your mind off of yourself and think about others!" Isn't that motherly wisdom? Yes, we need to have self-discipline in our food portions. We need to eat to be healthy. We need to make wise food choices and have self-control. But more than anything else, we—I, need to focus upward and outward instead of merely inward. It comes down to selfishness or self-centeredness. We must concentrate on being more selfless and focus on our steady growth in our faith and walk with the LORD instead. I learned that my skinny legs I really couldn't change. I am so thankful that God loves me just as I am, no matter how many times I let Him down. He is all-forgiving. God's unconditional love, and grace, and mercy, is the *why* I keep striving to love and worship Him more and more. God is abounding in goodness, patience, and forgives me again and again. His grace is sufficient.

My skinny legs don't consume me any longer. What does consume me is my passion for encouraging other women to stay in God's Word, to grow and hear His voice, while persevering through their trials and frustrations. To not give up. To have hope, joy, and peace found in the security of God's love, that can only be provided by our Lord.

But one has to believe in Him before it can transform one's life. As Romans 15:13 says, "May the God of hope fill you with all joy and peace in believing, so that by the power of the Holy Spirit, you may abound in hope." We must believe in what God says is true. Why do I doubt Him so many times? If God created me, and He is the perfect creator, then I was made for a purpose. That purpose was to glorify God in my life. I am here to serve God and be a shining light so that as it says in 1 Peter 2:12, "others may see my good deeds and glorify God on the day or times that the Holy Spirit prompts their hearts with His truth.

I continually have to shed my insecurity from my teenage years and put on God-confidence in how He made me. That is why I still prefer to wear my jeans or pants rather than dresses. My legs are then covered, and the problem solved. As it says in Psalm 139:14b, ". . . for I am fearfully and wonderfully made. Wonderful are your works; my soul knows it very well."

Look around you next time you go to church or are at work. Does someone look lonely? Do you see anyone who looks like they feel they don't belong? Who can you encourage and tell them that Christ cares about every inch of their existence?

⸭ Questions ⸭

1. Who has encouraged you in your life that stands out to you? How have they inspired and supported you?

2. Who can you reach out to uplift and give comforting words they are yearning to hear?

3. What has made you feel like quitting at times? What verse helped you have endurance and perseverance?

4. What part of your body that you previously hated can you thank God for as your creator?

4

Trusting While Searching For The Right Path

"Trust in the LORD with all your heart, and do not lean on your own understanding. In all your ways acknowledge him, and he will make your paths straight."

Proverbs 3:5-6

"You make known to me the path of life; in your presence there is fullness of joy; at your right hand are pleasures forevermore."

Psalm 16:11

Back in January 2016, my husband was searching for the right employment. He had owned a company that did not support a living any longer, so it had to be closed and dissolved. It seems to no longer be the norm in our culture today for people to have the same job all of their life. In today's society, it is more prevalent for people to have had more than one, two, or even three positions in their career years of working. It was tempting to look at others that have had only one fulfilling job in their long-term employment and wonder about the grass being greener and why this has not been the case in my home? But that is not the path that God has led us down. There have been many curves, detours, and sharp right turns along this road. By the way, did you know David had several different jobs before he became king? Yes, David worked through his different seasons in life, just like we have had to do as well!

The Message says in Romans 8:15, "This resurrection life you received from God is not a timid, grave-tending life. It's adventurously expectant, greeting God with a childlike, 'What's next, Papa?' God's Spirit touches our spirits and confirms who we really are." Yes, "What's next, Papa?" "I don't know about tomorrow. I just live from day to day, but I know who holds my future, and I know who holds my hand." That was the words to an old song we use to sing when I was a child. My uncle Ted sang that song beautifully and is singing it up in Heaven, no doubt right now. Yes, our life has not been timid or dull that God has walked with us through each step of the way. It has been an adventure.

Life has progressed as it does. God answered our prayers back in January 2016, in Steve needing employment. A man in the same business as my husband recommended Steve to two young gentlemen, to hire him for his experience and a definite need they had due to the successful growth of their company. Steve interviewed and became an employee before leaving the interview. God did provide and put the networking connections together as I had prayed, while the job search had gone on for several months, and I had asked God to place Steve in just the right employment. "What's next, Papa?" God answered. God provided. My prayer was watered, seeds sown, and now the grass has been starting to turn greener.

When your husband is out of work or not liking the job he has, it is very tempting to view other husbands in comparison, that appear to be fulfilled in their career and ask why that is not the case in your home? But wait, maybe God has been trying to teach your husband various character traits, and to make him more beneficial through each job he has had. My husband has gained tremendous experience in many areas in each position he has held. He has gained expertise in acoustical performing equipment, acoustic requirements in a performance venue, architectural design, accounting, estimating, construction, home repair, and leadership skills, amongst others. He has many skills today that he would not have had, had he not had the jobs in each corporation. The experience God gave him has given him the skill sets that are so vitally needed now and are an additional asset at where he has been employed currently for several years. He is also able to use his skills in serving a ministry in drawing and designing an orphanage that will be built overseas, for a missionary organization. God has pulled his talents all together and is being used in ways we had no idea would transpire.

Looking back, my husband and I are amazed at how Jehovah Jireh—God provided our prayer for his employment. God has richly blessed him where he is at today. I asked Steve just the other day, "Did you pray for a job right in the Industrial Park of our community years ago? I know that was what you had wanted, but nothing back then turned up?" It takes him all of ten to maybe fifteen minutes to drive to work! He said yes, he thought he had, but now it seems more of a memory of a dream that God has abundantly blessed and answered!

I learned from this experience that God is not a wish granter like a genie in a bottle. God has a sovereign plan. We have to put feet to our prayers, as my husband frequently says, but God is the great I am! God is the ultimate networker in fashioning just the right connections He intends for our well-being. I had to learn in a new way, to trust Romans 8:28, "And we know that for those that love God all things work together for good." I will be tested in getting that lesson over and over until I die.

My grass is not any greener. But it is my lawn that God has provided me to live temporarily in—it is not my permanent address. Heaven and eternity with my Saviour is my eternal and permanent residing place of residence at His appointed time of destination. Is it yours?

⁑ Questions ⁑

1. How has God worked out a Romans 8:28 situation for your good recently? Were you surprised?

2. Do you understand the Spiritual gifts God has given you? Think about how you can use them in your employment. Look at taking a free Christian DISC personality test. Christian DISC is a registered trademark of Arizona Christian Counseling LLC.

3. How can you be of benefit to others? Who comes to your mind? That is the success God wants you to have that will count for eternity.

5

Not What I Planned To Hear

"For the righteous will never be moved; he will be remembered forever. He is not afraid of bad news, his heart is firm, trusting in the LORD. His heart is steady, he will not be afraid until he looks in triumph on his adversaries."

Psalm 112:6-8

"But whoever listens to me will dwell secure and will be at ease, without dread of disaster."

Proverbs 1:33

It happened again. It was not what I had planned to hear. I came home after spending time with my beautiful sisters in Christ, preparing together with our next women's Bible study at church. We had just shared answers to prayers and burdens on our hearts before going our separate ways at the end of the evening. The video Bible study we had watched was all about putting on the armor of God. In Priscilla Shirer's "The Armor of God" first video lesson, she teaches that prayer activates the armor. She says that we all have a target on our back, and it is not from a human.

That one evening, I walked into the house. I put my book down on my table in my office and walked out and found my husband in his office in front of his computer, working on a quote for a client. The meeting with these dear women still exhilarated me. It was about ten o'clock at night and time to go to bed, or so I thought. Steve asked how the evening had gone, and then his next sentence stopped me: "Get ready for this. You want to know what has happened now?" He briefly told me the details of a very unpleasant situation that was now affecting us monetarily. The news was bad news. It wasn't fair, and it wasn't right. Once again, it was yet another disaster that was once still out of my husband's control that was taking us on another journey to have faith, hope, and trust in God. We were in another boat on the sea of life, and in a storm that had just broken out. Once again, we were humbled and seeking God for His provision and protection in this new trial. I confess I had thoughts about why was this happening? Why should we have to pay this bill that was not rightly ours? This was wrong! This was not right! This was terrible news!

When you hear bad news, isn't it reasonable to think or say, "Oh no, it can't be! You have to be kidding!" This was definitely in the wrong news category. I had just taught a women's Bible study this summer on handling trials in life without giving in to fear from my Bible study book I wrote called, "Taming The Lion's Roar. Handling Fear In The Midst Of A Trial." There were two main verses from my chapter two lesson: "Fear is Normal But Get Out of the Pit!" Psalm 112:6-8a was the first one: "For the righteous will never be moved; he will be remembered forever. He is *not afraid of bad news*; his heart is firm, trusting in the LORD. His heart is steady; he will not be afraid . . ." Then the second verse was from Proverbs 1:33, "But whoever listens to me will dwell secure and will be at ease *without dread of disaster*." I was thankful these very two verses came first into my mind. Next was to stand firm as 1 Corinthians 16:13 declares, "Be watchful, stand firm in the faith, act like men, be strong."

Once again, in another unexpected trial of life, we were determined to stand firm in our faith and conviction that God knew about this new disaster and, yes, terrible news, before we did. God has a plan. Like Dave Ramsey had told us in his "Financial Peace" class, and David in the Psalms, and Solomon in Proverbs, all have said, "OK, you have a problem. You will get through it. You have to figure out a plan of action and the solution and start it."

Was I afraid of the bad news? No. God had prepared me in reminding me about the precious verses in Psalm 112:6-8, and Proverbs 1:33 just taught by me a few weeks previously. I was determined not to give in to anxiety. I decided I would not compare myself to others that appeared to have it more comfortable than I did right then. My grass was not greener than yours, the reader. Your lawn was not greener than mine. God loves us both the same. God is our Shepherd. God is our shield. He has provided and protected me in the past, present, and will continue to do so in the future. My heart was firmly trusting in the LORD to work this out and somehow and in some way that I could not even imagine and fathom. So, I believed that God would work this out for our good somehow and in some, way.

When you fix your heart on the fear of the LORD, there is no need to fear the future. God promises to see us through. There will be dark times and dark days, but God is in control of it all. God saw Abraham through in providing a ram to sacrifice instead of Isaac. We read in Genesis 22:14, "So Abraham called the name of that place, "The LORD will provide"; as it is said to this day, "On the mount of the LORD it shall be provided."

I am still being educated in learning how to handle bad news in my life. God is still teaching me not to be *afraid* of disaster. He will hold me up in his secure love for me. God will not let me go!

It is now several years later. This apparent "bad news" my husband shared with me back in 2016, has not had a divine resolution that I can visibly see that it was for our good. Instead, I think it taught us wisdom in being cautious in business, and that God is Jehovah Jireh—God will provide. That is the point. It reminds me of 2 Corinthians 4:18 NLT, "So we don't look at the troubles we can see now; rather, we fix our gaze on things that cannot be seen. For the things we see now will soon be gone, but the things we cannot see will last forever." I let it go and placed it in God's hands to balance the scales as He divinely saw fit.

I need to check off from a list what God requires of me right now:

- Be hesitant in judging others (Matthew 7:1ff). Check?

- Pray for others that you feel have done you injustice (Matthew 5). Check?

- Never hold onto anger and quickly settle any hostile feelings (Matthew 5). Check?

- Allow God to defend and take revenge on our part (Matthew 5). Check?

- Continually forgive (Matthew 5) others. Forgiveness, even though not asked for, was a significant need in this "bad news." Check?

- Love (Matthew 5, 1 Corinthians 13:13; 2 Peter 1:7). Check?

·: Questions :·

1. What stories and lessons can you share in walking through life during "bad news" incidents in your ordinary everyday life? Did you fall into the trap of feeling that others had it more comfortable than you did? Was their grass greener than yours in a past bad news situation?

2. How has God provided for you during a "bad news" situation crisis in your life?

3. What trial has God taught you through that you can share with others in gaining comfort only you can give?

6

If Only I Could Be Perfect All Of The Time!

Psalm 19:7 tells us, "The law of the Lord is perfect, reviving the soul, the testimony of the Lord is sure, making wise the simple."

God's word is reliable, right, pure, holy, and accurate. It gives us needed CPR as it revives our soul. It is where we find strength in times of need. God's law shows us our imperfections.

The Greek word for perfect in Matthew 5:48 ("You therefore must be perfect, as your heavenly Father is perfect") means wanting nothing necessary to completeness; finished. That is a humanly impossible, unattainable attribute of God. He is perfect.

If we would all live as Jesus taught in Matthew 5, we would indeed be perfect. It would look like this:

- Always content no matter what our financial position.

- Always truthful to ourselves and others.

- Loving all people—even our enemies.

- Never hating anyone.

- Being a consistent shining light at all times, no matter what circumstances may distract us.

- Praying for our enemies.

- Never holding onto anger and quickly squelching any hostile feelings.

- Continually forgiving others without them asking us to forgive them.

How I fall so short looking at this list that Jesus taught in Matthew 5. I fail every day. I am not always content. I get in a stew about various incidents that seem to be unjust and not fair, especially within my workday experiences. Forgiveness is not the first thought that comes to my mind and settles into my heart and soul. I want to protect what is rightfully mine. But praise God, He loves me unconditionally and is rich in His mercy and grace.

None of us can attain perfection. However, God says He has set the bar in front of us all. I am helpless and hopeless, apart from God. BUT I am complete in Him. It is a process that never ends while we live on this earth.

Charles Spurgeon had said, "I recollect when I resolved never to sin again. I sinned before I had done my breakfast."

We are told in Psalm 18:30 (NLT), "God's way is perfect. All the LORD's promises prove true. He is a shield to all who look to him for protection." God's way will always be perfect.

1 Corinthians 13:12 (NLT) states, "Now we see things imperfectly, like puzzling reflections in a mirror, but then we will see everything with perfect clarity. All that I know now is partial and incomplete, because I do not know the how and why. But then I will know everything completely, just as God now knows me completely." Yes, we cannot see into the future and understand our current circumstances most often. But someday, when we get to glory, we will be able to understand it all. When we are in heaven, answers to our questions will be crystal clear.

Many things that bothered us on this earth won't matter any longer when we arrive up in heaven. As Revelation 21:4 declares, "He will wipe away every tear from their eyes, and death shall be no more, neither will there be mourning, nor crying, nor pain anymore, for the former things have passed away." No more tears. No more pain. Just pure joy when we are in Heaven!

As we start to look at what true contentment is, may we reflect, analyze, and scrutinize where we have grown and matured in Christ. Some things are now in the past and need to stay there. Release old hurts and resolve not to have a more extended look in the rearview mirror of your life.

Be renewed in Christ day by day. Be quick to forgive and love others. Abide in Him. Let your light radiate the presence of the King of Kings and Lord of Lord's.

As Jude 1:24a declares, "Now to him who is able to keep you from stumbling and to present you blameless before the presence of his glory with great joy . . ."

Blameless? That is another definition of being perfect. We all need to have complete trust and hope in the sufficiency of Christ. Have 2 Peter 1:5-7 be your legacy, "Make every effort to supplement your faith with virtue, and to virtue with knowledge, and to knowledge self-control, and to self-control with steadfastness, and to steadfastness with godliness, and to godliness with brotherly affection, and to brotherly affection, with love. For if these qualities are yours and are increasing, they keep you from being ineffective or unfruitful in the knowledge of our Lord Jesus Christ."

That is quite a list of supplements needed to be added to one's faith. Yet if we keep our thoughts more on developing these qualities in our lives, we won't be looking at anyone else's grass, and it won't matter.

⸵ Questions ⸵

1. Read 1 Corinthians 10:31: "So whether you eat or drink, or whatever you do, do all to the glory of God." How can that verse help you deal with feelings of failure?

2. Ask God to make you of benefit in your job, your family, within your circle of friends. Then watch in anticipation for your grass to turn greener.

3. How much time do you devote to prayer? Is it sufficient? What needs to be changed?

7

Do You Really Know Jesus Christ?

W̲e, women, need to focus our minds more on Christ than ourselves. There, I said it. That is part of our problem with insecurity and comparing ourselves with one another and feel we are lacking. We have a sinful nature. But we are anointed, redeemed, and His child, if we have accepted Christ as our Savior. We strive to be perfect, and we fall short. Our problem is we need to know Christ Jesus more intimately rather than comparing what Sally has compared to what we have in life.

A few names we find in Scripture for Jesus are:

- Prince of Peace.
- Son of the most high.
- Shepherd.
- Redeemer.

- Son of the living God.
- God in the flesh.
- Our Savior.
- Messiah.
- Lamb of God.
- Emmanuel, God with us.
- Jehovah, my God.
- I am.
- Creator of all things.
- Alpha and Omega, the beginning and the end.
- The Light of the world.

Do you really know who Jesus is? Do you believe Him? Throughout the gospels, Jesus responded to people who didn't have much faith. Jesus just wants us to believe He is who He says He is. The Lord wants us to have heart knowledge and not just head knowledge. He wants us to have no doubts that He can if He chooses.

Are you listening to the Lord's voice? Are you drenched in His Word daily, so you are armed against Satan and his army? When I get up in the morning, I ask Him: "OK, Jesus, what do You want to say to me today? What do You want me to understand?" as I open my Bible and get out my journal and prayer journal. Next, I write out my plans for the day. But I put a question mark next to the heading: "My Plans For Today—God?" I am asking God if He approves of my plans. I want Him to bless them or redirect me to what He intends for my day to be. Now with the COVID-19 pandemic, my sales job has changed somewhat. I have added Proverbs 16:3 above my list for the day as well, which says, "Commit your work unto the LORD and your plans will b be established." I need God to bring about connections with new customers and institute agreements in my sales endeavors for my workplace as specific changes and hindrances have occurred due to COVID-19. The following morning I look at the previous day's plans I had listed and am amazed at how it has changed, or the distractions have rearranged what I had set out to do that day. Or something that I had thought was of great importance turned out not to be necessary. I love how God redirects the circumstances for my protection and my best since He is my Shepherd and Overseer.

Last year I had chosen to read the one red-letter Bible that I own, to learn everything that Jesus Christ said. I studied all the printed words that are in red. I was, of course, reading the verses around the red printed verses, so I understood the context and the setting. This was my tool to know better what He wants to say to me through His Word. I wanted to grow in the knowledge of Jesus, by reading what He specifically said before His death and resurrection into Heaven. I could then know and grasp the words that He said in the gospels better.

I have since then moved through the books in the New Testament and am currently in 1 Corinthians. I want to be ready to hear His voice to me as precious verses jump off the page at me and grab me when I read the Word of God. I want to have my heart and mind equipped to have my shield of faith up by planting the truths of my Savior in my soul, from what He spoke while on this earth, fulfilling God's purpose of a redeeming Savior. He was the Lamb of God who came to seek and to save as Luke 19:10 says: "For the Son of Man is come to seek and to save, that which was lost."

If I stop developing spiritually, my life becomes barren, and I become blind to my real condition. That is when I start to compare myself with other sisters in Christ again and get insecure and not have true contentment. But it is such a habit, and bad habits need to be broken!

I have to ask myself daily: Am I content with my knowledge of Jesus Christ? How can I learn more about Him, and what is found in God's Word? I need to tell God more often how much I love Him! That would keep me from feeling inadequate and a failure. The more I grow in knowing my Saviour, the more I am less significant. I have to keep doing this over and over as it is a continual work in progress in my walk with the Lord. We must remember whose we are and, therefore, who we are.

⁝ Questions ⁝

1. Are your what-ifs holding you back? Take courage. Your heavenly Father is cheering you on!

2. Write down a list of the attributes of God. Which one has God shown to you the most this week?

3. Do you learn more about Jesus from the trials or your successes? What is your go-to verse when facing troubles reminding you of God's overseeing love and care?

8

But I Don't Fit In

Recently, with the current political atmosphere, I have felt I don't fit in with various groups of people. The left is very unrelenting in not being genuinely open-minded and indeed are not tolerant when others give an opposing opinion. They expound on the importance of being tolerant in society, yet they don't live it themselves. It becomes very one-sided.

When I am criticized, I feel like I am back in junior high. I feel unaccepted. I think I don't fit in. I feel like something is wrong with me, and I am now an outsider. I have a fear of not being good enough. I feel rejection. Do you ever think that way too? But that is one of the many ways Satan attacks all perfectionists, of which I am one. Why is it so important to feel loved, wanted, and admired? That is a basic need we all have, but it can also become an idol.

How does the enemy attack you? Have you thought about that? We are all a walking target; Satan is waiting to pounce on with his weapons of guilt, shame, frustration, and feelings of failure. Those can be fears that get out of control if we harbor those thoughts too long. I continually beat myself up with remorse and regret after the fact of many conversations I have had with friends. I later review in my head the responses I have said and shrink in deep remorse. I say to myself, "How could I have said that? She must think I am terrible! She must think I am a horrible Christian. How could I have said that in reply? She will never like me again!"

We need to draw very close to the Lord and stand firm in our faith when fighting insecurity in comparing ourselves to anyone else. But Satan does his craftiness in pulling us away from God rather than toward Him. I will not let him win! That arrow in my back is not going to be a permanent fixture. I have ammunition to fight back with verses that are the promises of God that are eternal and available at all times. God keeps telling us He's got this! Don't forget you are a daughter of the king made in His image. He is your heavenly father. He is your shepherd and overseer.

James 4:7-8 declares: "Submit yourselves therefore to God. Resist the devil, and he will flee from you. Draw near to God, and he will draw near to you." That is the antidote. That is the needed action to implement.

God just requires my obedience to Him. It only takes a mustard seed of faith. It doesn't have to be equal to the size of a pail or swimming pool. No, God just asks me to trust Him to do what He says He will do. He will take care of the rest.

But I am a people pleaser. Are you? We think we have to be the be-all to everyone. Conflict is our enemy. We have to keep peace at all costs; otherwise, we feel that someone will not like us. That is our primary concern. Everyone has to be our friend, or something is wrong with us—people pleasers.

Words of encouragement are our soothingly received love language. The tone of someone else's words is critical. It causes us to have a good day or a bad day. Do you have days like that too?

When men walk into a room, they just look for a familiar face or someone that makes eye contact with them for engaging in conversation. However, we women see over the faces in the room and usually look for someone we already know. But sometimes I will see over the sea of faces for someone who looks lonely. I gravitate more to that woman because I know what it feels like to feel alone, and I want to be the solution to anyone that has that emotion at a particular time or place and maybe hurting. I am a fixer. I am generally outgoing and friendly, and yet I may draw inward in a crowd. I am much better on a one to one basis with conversation than amongst a group of people.

When I was in high school, I suffered much from insecurity. I grew up in a small town and attended a high school that had 110 students in my graduating class. I was raised in a German heritage family that often did not acknowledge feelings. Older family members being German, tended to think crying was a sign of weakness. They suppressed feelings. They did not learn how to deal with emotions. When my one aunt of 40 some years died abruptly from cancer, my grandmother never openly cried. My dad did, and his other siblings did, however. They managed to be black and white. I didn't fit in with that.

I always cared very deeply and had a longing need to be told I did "very good" instead of being told I was "pretty good" during my childhood and into adulthood. I was brought up with the philosophy that one must remain humble and not be prideful, and to do that saying what you accomplished was "pretty good" was considered a compliment. But I needed to hear the phrase, "My oh my! You did that very well!" So because of that upbringing, I craved compliments. My glass was usually half empty rather than half full when I then became an adult in my mindset or view of things.

What was your upbringing like—anything similar? Then you also suffer from looking at another's grass as being greener because you are holding your life's glass as being viewed as half-empty too. You find your life is not quite good enough.

You are not content.

Dear sister, repeat after me:

God dearly loves me.

He made me for a purpose.

He gave me talents and gifts that are needed, and no one else can do them but by me.

I was born into the family that God created for them and me.

God does not make mistakes. I do, but they do not define me.

Tomorrow is a new day given to me by God. I will rejoice and be glad in it!

My grass may not be as green as yours, but it is not brown. It just needs God's constant watering of truth in front of each step and breath that I take as I focus solely on Jesus Christ and all that He has done for me, instead of what I have done.

⁙ Questions ⁙

1. What can you do when you are in a setting of people that you feel you don't fit in? What questions can you think to ask them to create conversation and bonding?

2. When you walk into a church function, observe the room and pick out someone who looks like they need someone to talk to them. Then ask what they are reading in their Bible currently? Ask how you can pray for them?

3. How can you listen to others better? Who can you show interest to that you have not demonstrated to before that you might have ignored unknowingly?

9

Target On My Back

We that are believers in Christ all have a target on our back. This is true, especially for anyone in ministry, which is not only done in a church setting. "Work is worship" is not just a saying—it is a reality. God created work as a gift. He intends us to use our spiritual gifts within our work to be of benefit to the company we work for, as all work is sacred work. Satan wants to keep the truth from being spread. He will do all he can to squelch the passions of proclaiming that Jesus is the only way, the truth, and the life, due to discouragement!

I have discovered that one of the enemy's attacks against me is words of criticism. That quickly discourages me and is a temptation I have to fight against continually. Is it yours? I tend to be a perfectionist, although I hate to admit it. I love to read self-help books. Books that are more in the non-fiction category than just everyday fiction novels. I am always reviewing how I can do everything better. I look at other women and think they have it all together much better than I often do. There I go again—the comparison trap.

Satan has been working harder recently at trying to put a dividing wedge in a personal area in my life. Just when I am writing, teaching, or focusing on a particular subject matter of scripture, he shoots at my relationship with my husband, or people I work within my job. I get caught unaware and wonder where did this come from or how? Why did this happen? Are other couples at church going through these crazy cycles too? Are other women in the workforce having relationship problems in their workplace also?

I continue to write and post my women's devotional Blog, www.lindavanlohkillian.com. My Blog is called "Devotional Fuel Pulls to Reboot Your Mind." I write a weekly devotional on what I have been studying from the Bible during the week. Currently, I just finished 2 Corinthians. I give a quick (I try to keep it under 500 words), direct focus on rebooting our minds with the truths found in scripture and applying it to our daily lives and especially to fellow women that are in the workplace. We, women, are living real life in a culture that we don't always fit in, but we must stay encouraged by reading God's Word and applying it to everyday life. Our spirituality in Christ must not be compartmentalized. Living out our Christianity is not supposed to only happen on Sundays. It is to be integrated into every part of our life. We all need to reboot our minds and fill it with the truth of God's Word because life does get messy. My blog's weekly content is usually based on something behind the scenes in my own life, a friend's life, or someone within my family that God shows me as an illustration of the portion of Scripture I have been studying during the week, in applying it to my own life. So many activities within our family, work, and church keep us so busy with being busy. We all need reminders to be aware and remember Jesus is walking right beside us every step of the way as we invite Him into our sales call, work meeting, or simply riding in the passenger seat of our car in driving to work.

We read about Jesus walking right beside us in Psalm 23. Did you realize that means Jesus is following, guiding, leading, and nudging you because He is walking the same road you are on right beside you? I have to remind myself of that fact day by day, as Matthew 28:20b tells us, "I am with you always, to the end of the age."

A fellow worker asked me how my book was coming? I realized I had stopped because the writing juices had been put on hold due to having feelings of insecurity. Can you believe that? My writing project on the problem with comparing ourselves to others, and I was afraid it might not be good enough! There were several instances of conflict that also became a trap I fell into in feeling inadequate and a failure in several work instances. That is the oxymoron of oxymorons! Will anyone identify with me? Will women want to read it? But I know I have so much more to say here as I continue to grow in this area. Will I ever grow up in this female dilemma of the comparison trap? I seem to go two steps forward, and then crash, and the target on my back has a sharp arrow that has hit me right in the center at the bullseye! I then have to pause and re-read verses of Scripture God has blessed my heart and instructed me with in the past. Life then stops for a bit.

So have I conquered not comparing myself and even looking at some other woman and wanting what she has instead? No. Not all the time. But I continue to work at growing in the Lord, one day at a time. One step at a time. Becoming more holy in the Spirit's work is what life is really all about. We that know the Lord are called to a higher calling of being a light for the gospel of Christ. Some plant seeds and others water. We sometimes need to remind ourselves that living on this earth will not last forever.

How do you respond to criticism? Do you always say thank you I needed to hear that? Or simply nod, smile, and walk away? The question really is, what am I trusting in to make me happy? Why is this person's opinion sending me off the cliff? Has being accepted become an idol? Are people responsible for my happiness, or is God's love for me and His protection, shield, and comfort sufficient?

The assignment I have given myself now is to echo my praise of thanksgiving to God every day from His Word. Psalm 145:1-3 is my echo, "I will extol you my God and king, and bless your name for ever and ever. Every day I will bless you and praise your name forever and ever. Great is the LORD, and greatly to be praised, and his greatness is unsearchable."

We, women, have to calm our racing minds and thoughts of discontentment consistently. We have to talk to ourselves and sometimes just do it out loud. My grass is not any greener. Your lawn is not any greener than mine on your side of the fence. Let's just focus on Christ's sacrifice, power, compassion, justice, mercy, grace, sovereignty, righteousness, and our relationship with Him. That needs to be our primary focus. All the rest will then fall into place. My lawn is not any greener. No one else's grass is any greener either. Our worth and identity is in Christ alone. Insecurity leads to discouragement and folly. God's resources are bountiful. We must crave and seek God's approval over any human's. Psalm 119:18 declares, "Open my eyes that I may behold wondrous things out of your law."

So take Satan's arrow off the target on your back and fill the holes with precious promises from Psalms, the gospels, Hebrews, and many other books of the Bible. Immerse your heart and mind in the truths of scripture that will squelch the target of despair and instead refill your soul from the fountain of life.

Make a list of all the names for God. My favorite is Jehovah Jireh—the LORD will provide. Another is Jehovah Shammah—ever-present one. What about His nature can you see in these names?

What idols are you carrying around?

Whose evaluation of you counts for eternity? God's or someone else?

Flee to Jesus! Remember how Joseph fled from Pharaoh's wife to escape temptation? He ran and got out of the house (Genesis 39:12)! When you are tempted to dig yourself into a pit and throw in all of your mistakes and failures in a heaping pile – run instead into the compassionate and unconditional love of Jesus. Examine what you did wrong, confess the sin and ask God's forgiveness, and learn from the error, so you don't make that wrong choice again. Then thank God for the green pastures He has given you. Be passionate about reading and learning from God's Word. It is your light, and God wants you to shine that light before others. God has given you something to do that shows who God is through the spiritual gifts He has freely bestowed upon you by His Holy Spirit. God wants you to use your leadership skills, encouragement skills, understanding application of knowledge from God found in His Word, giving you supernatural insight and higher wisdom in handling work conflicts, or to solve a problem. Are you blessed by having the gift of faith? We all must have faith, but the gift of faith is the unique ability to trust God against all circumstances, just like Peter did when he got out of the boat and walked on water.

⁝ Questions ⁝

1. How can you train your heart and mind to look for God at work in your life?

2. How does acknowledging God's presence change the way you live each day?

3. Do you need to refocus and reflect on what God is giving you to do that shows who God is?

10
Filled To Full Capacity

The definition of the word "fullness" is containing all that is wanted, needed, or possible—not needing anything more—that state of being filled to capacity, complete, lacking nothing.

Paul states in Ephesians 3:19, "and to know the love of Christ that surpasses knowledge, that you may be *filled* with all the *fullness of God*."

This verse was part of a prayer Paul prayed while he was in prison, for the people in the church at Ephesus. Paul founded this church. He prays for the Holy Spirit's power to strengthen the hearts of these believers and for them to comprehend the immense love of Christ. Paul's burden was for these individuals to use the resources available to them, which are grace, mercy, power, and love, laid up in Jesus Christ. The same is true for us today. Through God's empowering Spirit, we are complete. The

Holy Spirit is the immediate worker of grace in the souls of God's people. We have *all* the fullness of God obtainable and accessible to us at *all* times.

The Greek word *Epignosis* means precise and correct knowledge of God. It is having divine wisdom, intimate, personal, and experiential knowledge of God and Christ. Paul so wanted these believers to have this type of awareness of the love of Christ for everyone—Jew or Gentile. It involves realizing if you are a Christian, a Christ-follower, then you have overflowing and abundant ownership of Christ's love. God wants us to experience His fullness. He gives us gifts and graces and mercy, for He sees what we need.

The AMP text of Ephesians 3:19 says it best, "And (that you may come) to know (practically, through personal experience) the love of Christ which far surpasses (mere) knowledge (without experience), that you may be filled up (throughout your being) to all the fullness of God (so that you may have the richest experience of God's presence in your lives, completely filled and flooded with God Himself)."

Take out of your cupboard a glass measuring cup. Set it out in front of you on the counter and give yourself an object lesson. The Holy Spirit fills us up (looking at a glass measuring cup) with abundant comfort and knowledge of God due to His immense love for us. That is the source of real joy and peace. That is the picture inside of you of God filling you up with His love, joy, peace, and freedom in Christ.

If you are a Christian, you are already complete in Christ due to His grace.

Four verses regarding God's Grace:

- 2 Corinthians 12:9: "But he said to me, "My grace is sufficient for you, for my power is made perfect in weakness." Therefore I will boast all the more gladly of my weaknesses, so that the power of Christ may rest upon me."

- Ephesians 2:8: "For by grace you have been saved through faith. And this is not a result of works, so that no one may boast."

- James 4:6: "But he gives more grace. Therefore it says, "God opposes the proud, but gives grace to the humble."

- 2 Peter 1:2-3: "May grace and peace be multiplied to you in the knowledge of God and Jesus our Lord. His divine power has granted to us all things that pertain to life and godliness, through the knowledge of him who called us to his own glory and excellence."

Now, look at Colossians 2:9-10 which further declares, "And you have been filled in him, who is the head of all rule and authority." Think of yourself as a measuring cup, and that measuring cup is already full of water. It is complete. Nothing more needs to go into it, because the Holy Spirit is the means of our fullness in God.

James 1:4 also states, "And let steadfastness have its full effect, that you may be *perfect and complete*, lacking in *nothing*."

God grants us grace, giving us what we do not deserve. It is a gift. It never depends on our efforts or works. It is all from God. Do I get it? God has granted me all things that pertain to life and godliness. God's grace is given to me to set me on the right path. I just have to be aware that God is divinely orchestrating His plan for my life because He loves me. I only must be obedient in my faith, hope, and trust in my Heavenly Father.

Paul prayed, in Ephesians 3, for the believers to know Christ's love abundantly so they would be filled spiritually with the fullness of Him. He was not talking about some ecstatic or emotional experience. He was talking about God's holiness and glory. The Holy Spirit is given to us at the time of our accepting Christ as our Savior. The Holy Spirit is God in us transforming our lives.

God's power has been demonstrated by:

- Raising Jesus Christ from the dead. Mark 16:5-7.

- Seating Christ at the right hand of God. Ephesians 1:20.

- By grace, giving salvation to those who accept and believe in Jesus Christ. Ephesians 2:5-6.

- Our eternal life is with Christ, sitting "in the heavenly realms." Ephesians 1:3. That is where our spiritual blessings come from and where our final spiritual home will be. Spiritual benefits are not from Christ but in Christ.

We have this same power living within our soul. God says, draw near to me and I will draw near to you (James 4:8).

May we realize the fullness of God's love in our lives and not let insecurities squelch our potential for living an abundant life in Christ. I am not talking about "name it and claim it" or earthly prosperity false teachings. *We are complete in Him through His grace.* May we meditate on growing in the knowledge of Christ's love for us and the fullness of His power from the grace He freely gives to us.

Warren Wiersbe has said, "We are so rich in Christ that our riches cannot be calculated even with the most sophisticated computer . . . No Christian ever has to worry about having inadequate spiritual resources to meet the demands of life."

So I ask myself, why do I get so knotted up from the drama and conflicts at work? God has given me everything I need. Therefore I am complete in Christ. God is my shepherd, my overseer, my shield of protection. So then why does it matter when criticisms hurt and cause me to fall to the temptation of feeling inferior and insufficient? The grass over on the other side of the fence tempts me to think it is greener than my own. I have to go back and check myself if I am battling guilt, shame, frustration, or failure. Those are the weapons of the enemy, and Jesus never belittles me because it says in the Bible He loves me, and therefore He adores me! 1 John 1:3, states, " See what kind of love the Father has given to us, that we should be called the children of God; and so we are." You adore your children, so think about that emotion and apply it to God's love in turn for you as His child, His daughter! That makes me giggle in gratitude! How about you?

ꞏ Questions ꞏ

1. Whose evaluation of you is more important? God or the opinion of others?

2. What truth has God taught you this week about His faithfulness, grace, or mercy?

3. What verse reminds you that complete joy is found only in Christ?

11
Craving Righteousness

*"Blessed are those who hunger and thirst for righteousness,
for they shall be satisfied."*
Matthew 5:6

Do you spend much time craving righteousness? How do you define that? What does it really mean?

Righteousness is a lifestyle. It does not mean following a set of rules and traditions—that is, legalism. Instead, it is living in complete obedience to Christ, having faithful perseverance, and putting Him first above anything else. Righteousness has to do with attitudes and intents of the heart, not just conduct. It has to do with character. It distinguishes a true Christian, a Christ-follower, instead of following the world's culture and philosophy.

Romans 12:1-2 is a good description of what righteousness means: "I appeal to you, therefore, brothers, by the mercies of God to present your bodies as a living sacrifice, holy and acceptable to God, which is your spiritual worship. Do not be conformed to this world, but be transformed by the renewal of your mind, that by testing you may discern what the is the will of God, what is good and acceptable and perfect."

When you are thirsty and dehydrated, the tongue will stick to the roof of your mouth due to a lack of saliva. You have an intense desire, intense craving, and an intensely focused pursuit of finding satisfaction from drinking Gatorade or perhaps Coconut Water to replace the electrolytes lost in your body. It is with that same kind of intensity and passion that the believer needs to pursue righteousness.

Jesus promised fulfillment in Matthew 5:6b when He said, "for they shall be satisfied." Does that mean you will get that promotion, long life, perfect marriage, perfect children, and excellent friends from pursuing righteousness? No. So what then? If you seek to have a Christ-honoring lifestyle, it starts with your heart that is changed from the inside out. But you have to want it. It takes passion. It takes determination.

Craving righteousness requires:

- Eagerly pursuing a consistent life of honoring Christ in all things.

- Putting a priority on spending time in prayer

and giving thanks to God for all of the many blessings He has given.

- Righteousness holds God's will to be at the highest level of importance, producing His power in our lives (Matthew 7:21).

- You are no longer seeking praise first from your spouse, friends, fellow employees, but seeking God's approval above anyone else. Ouch. But that is what craving righteousness is all about.

- You know yourself, accepting yourself, and being yourself to the glory of God.

- Confessing sin immediately be it anger, bitterness, envy, lack of contentment, grumbling, gossip—whatever it is, squelching it quickly.

Having humility over pride is a balance we must pursue. It requires power under control. Then showing forgiveness and mercy to others as God has shown mercy to you (Matthew 9:13).

Right now, I am sitting at my computer, staring at the screen, and rereading these words. My arms are bent, elbows are on my desk, and my chin is resting on my hands. God continues to impress upon me my need for having a humble heart. I have such a long way to go!

We all need compliments, don't misunderstand what I am saying. I so appreciate encouraging comments about my women's devotional blog, "Devotional Pulls to Reboot Your Mind." I need encouragement, too, when I have bled and poured out my heart on printed paper and the web, revealing my vulnerability. But we should not crave and only live for the applause of others.

We can enjoy being appreciated but not live, so to *crave* it. That is the difference.

Acts of kindness can change someone's whole day with just a longing and spontaneous kind word or compliment. That is how we lift each other up by making much of others rather than merely ourselves—looking at our glass half full instead of half empty. Again, this is yet another area where I have a lot of work to do.

As Paul said when he faced death calmly in 2 Timothy 4:7-8, "I have fought the good fight, I have finished the race, I have kept the faith. Now there is in store for me the crown of righteousness, which the Lord, the righteous judge, will award to me on that day—and not only to me, but to all who have longed for his appearing." Dear Jesus, come quickly!

How can you be more effective today for Christ than you were yesterday?

The same passionate drive and ambitions that are needed in winning at sports, excelling in a sales job, being an active leader, or maybe just wanting to be the best at something are what is likewise needed in pursuing righteousness. When we are spiritually hungry, God feeds us through His Word. But we must read it for us to know Him. He gives to all the invitation: "Come everyone who thirsts ... Seek the LORD while he may be found; call upon him while he may be near." Isaiah 55:1, 6.

We have to answer the question, do I crave the approval of God more than anyone else?

Matthew 5:6 NIV declares: "Blessed are those who hunger and thirst for righteousness, for they will be filled."

Make craving God's righteousness your passion and thirst today rather than dwelling on someone else's lawn that is not any greener than yours.

⁙ Questions ⁙

1. What is your definition of righteousness?

2. What are you passionate about? How is God a part of that passion?

3. Is seeking complements your focus in accomplishing a project?

12

Manumit

[man-*yuh*-mit]
verb (used with object) to release from slavery

One morning I received in my Outlook email a Word Of The Day from Miriam Webster's site that instructs one on a definition of a word not commonly used and gives the history and how to use the word in a sentence. It is a literary tool in building one's vocabulary. The word "manumit" appeared, and I could immediately see a correlation for this term I had never heard of before within my Christian life from its meaning. The definition said it meant to be released from slavery. To be set free. Don't we all have various circumstances throughout our day that hold us in bondage where we need to be set free? Yet in Psalm 25:20-21, David prayed, "Oh, guard my soul, and deliver me! Let me not be put to shame, for I take refuge in you. May integrity and uprightness preserve me, for I wait for you."

A few daily adrenalin depleting stresses may be:

- Did I let my children down?

- Did I let my boss down in my response or how I handled a situation?

- Did I perform well enough at my presentation at work or a ministry teaching spot?

- Will my children remember more of the good things from their childhood rather than the mistakes I made as a parent?

- Is anyone praying for me?

- Why can't I make everyone get along?

- How could I have said that? They must think I am terrible!

Care to admit any of your own regrets?

When we are bogged down by the circumstances in our day that are like pebbles in our shoe, and like a paper cut, we become enslaved and in captivity to them. God is always there to release us from the bondage of fears, our misgivings, and pressures of life. Why do we carry the load we were never intended to take? As Jesus said in John 8:31-32, "If you abide in my word, you are truly my disciples, and you will know the truth, and truth will set you free." We are set free by the truth of God's Word and His grace!

We, women, need to let go of the self-induced problem of our comparison trap. We have made ourselves slaves to our ego, which will then always produce insecurity. That is the apparent result. We have to break the chain and reboot our minds to look up at God first, rather than comparing ourselves with one another's gifts or talents God has given individually to each one of us. God does not make or need duplicates. We must stop being slaves to craving recognition from anyone other than the Lord God Himself.

Are you carrying around a ball and chain that is holding you down? That is called a stronghold in Christian circles. Insecurity and having to be perfect all the time is a weight that many of us carry around, and we don't even recognize it. We waste time with unnecessary fears that we are not good enough.

James 1:4 states, "And let steadfastness have its full effect, that you may be perfect and complete, lacking in nothing." James uses the word "complete." I think of what complete means—nothing lacking. That's it—it is finished—done—something made whole or perfect. Seeing God's faithfulness in our lives frees us from the slavery of comparing ourselves to others and gives us hope.

I have to ask myself, who is more important to please—God or people? That answer is obvious—my obedience to God is of the utmost importance. Improvement can always be made with any subject or any effort. But worrying about the final delivery should be placed in God's hands for safekeeping. Oh, how I need to remind myself of this.

We all worry about so many things. We are bombarded all day with Satan's targets, traps, and snars to trip us up. I picture myself driving a bumper car on the race track of life. I feel I have to drive faster and smarter to get ahead of any other bumper cars on my route. Then I have to make sure I don't have a collision with any additional drivers. I have to be first to the finish line. That is called having a competitive nature. It is also called being a perfectionist. Both can cause me to become a slave to either one. What enslaves you?

I have 1 Peter 5:7 printed and hanging on the front of my office desk, "Casting all your anxieties on Him, because He cares for you." It is a picture of a man casting out his line into a lake he is standing in. That vivid picture of casting out a fishing line, like casting out to God all of your worries, insecurities, imperfections, and telling Him He can take them. That is what it takes every day and all day long. It has to happen day after day, and over and over again, as 1 Thessalonians 5:16, states we are to "pray without ceasing." It might mean praying one hundred times or even three hundred times until God takes away the difficulty—until He supplies the answers to what you are asking or lets you know that His grace is sufficient for you to bear the pain or the disappointment, as he did with Paul.

There are no shortcuts in being released from the slavery of the comparison trap. But we have to retrain our minds from God's Word that His grace is sufficient for us, and His mercies are new every morning! Our sufficiency is in Christ and nothing else.

There was a picture that hung in my bedroom when I was a very young child. I can still see it in my mind, hanging on my bedroom wall. It was the picture of Jesus knocking on someone's front door. It is called The Light of the Word painting and was completed in 1853, by William Hollman Hunt. It illustrates Revelation 3:20, "Behold, I stand at the door and knock. If anyone hears my voice and opens the door, I will come in to him and eat with him, and he with me." What I didn't know was that this door does not have a handle on the outside. It can only be opened from the inside. It depicts Christ knocking on the door of a soul that is lost in the darkness of ignorance and wilfulness. But there is an opening of a grillwork on the door, revealing the darkness and so that the individual on the inside may see who is knocking at the door is good and kind. This painting is premised on one's acceptance of Jesus calling one to be "born again" and of His steadfast love. Others interpret this to be a picture of the freedom of the will. The importance of this painting was that there was no door or latch on the outside of the door. It had to be opened from the inside depicting Jesus Christ knocking at one's heart's door and should not be ignored.

Salvation through Jesus Christ alone comes as Ephesians 2:4 states, "But God, being rich in mercy, because of the great love with which he loves us, even when we were dead in our trespasses made us alive together with Christ—by grace you have been saved – and raised us up with him, and seated us with him in the heavenly places in Christ Jesus so that in the coming ages he might show the immeasurable riches of his grace in kindness toward us in Christ Jesus."

Jesus made us alive in Christ at the time of our accepting Him as our Saviour. We are alive with Christ. I can't wait to see His throne! I am going to get to sit with Him in heavenly places! I need to think about that more than wishing I had more wit, more creativity, more intelligence, or more awards of achievements. That is what counts in this world. Not the size of the house I live in or what car I drive. Not if I did anything perfect or not. I am promised immeasurable riches of His grace in kindness towards me! I need to dwell and meditate on that rather than if my grass is greener than yours. Let us shed the chains of slavery of not feeling good enough, smart enough, or popular enough when we have sincerely and humbly done our best. That is all God asks of us. Remember the word manumit and its meaning, and then apply it in your Christian walk.

⁊ Questions ⁊

1. When you get to heaven, will God be able to tell you, "Well done, thou good and faithful servant?"

2. What is the sin that so quickly has you in slavery?

3. What is the last thing you did that made you feel totally embarrassed? Why were you embarrassed? Does it matter now whatever this was that took place in the past?

God has provided for you. Rest in that spot. Read Psalm 25 and pray those words as David did and is known and called a man after God's own heart. He made mistakes and fell into sin, but he quickly accepted responsibility and humbly repented.

The goal and challenge is to become more like Christ and be a mirror of Jesus at all times one day at a time. Will that change anything you do today?

May the Lord fill your heart and soul with the freedom of His peace and hope, giving you needed perseverance for whatever may try to hold you, hostage, next. The trial may not yet have its end, but the peace of God gives liberation.

13

Smokescreen

"Now after John was arrested, Jesus came into Galilee, proclaiming the gospel of God, and saying, "The time is fulfilled, and the kingdom of God is at hand, repent and believe in the gospel."

Mark 1:14-15

I was sitting across the table at a MacDonald's with a man that was a new supplier in my sales job. Their products are for benefiting and improving hair and skincare products. He wanted to meet together over coffee, after we finished our joint sales calls together, calling on research and development chemists, showing this new product line to them. I was curious about his accent and didn't recognize which country it would have originated from. He told me he was from Israel and informed me of many things I did not know about the nation Israel. I was intrigued. I mentioned that I was curious about the Egyptian culture vs. Israel's culture because I had just read in the Bible of Joseph telling his brothers not to say to the Pharaoh that they were shepherds because the Egyptians looked down at shepherds. Instead, he told them to say they overlooked livestock; then, they would appear better before the king. But this man who I had just finished making joint sales calls together, discounted Jesus as the Messiah, and stated his reasons. He believed in God and held to conservative positions in politics, but he denied that Jesus was the Messiah. He said dogmatically why. To me, that seemed more of an opinion than any proven fact.

I had to go home then and do research. So I typed into Google: "Jews discounting Jesus riding on a donkey," which was his reasoning. It lead me to a website called Jews for Jesus, and a woman immediately appeared through a chat place to the right of the contents. She chatted with me online about my conversation with him. She quickly stated: "It is a smokescreen—what he disclaimed about the words in translation of the Bible. It was his way to avoid talking about having his sins being able to be forgiven by Jesus!" That was a new realization to me of various "smokescreens" people put up to get around realizing the simple truth of the gospel. I had left feeling I hadn't done a good enough job in sharing Christ with this man, that it was all my fault, and I determined to do a better job at it the next time we worked together. That was another step that God used to impress upon me the need to start a new ministry at our church, which we call the Fellowship Of Women In The Workplace. It encourages

Christian women to learn what a woman's unique contribution to the workplace is, and it is time for us women to navigate and lead like Jesus effectively and confidently. Stopping the comparison trap requires us to have tools for uniquely leading and influencing those we work with throughout the day as we recognize we are in the presence of Jesus and to abide and rest in His presence. This ministry also focuses on how to effectively show your faith during your day to day work responsibilities. It doesn't necessarily mean you share the Romans Road plan or John 3:16 every time. Relationships and trust must first be formed. Showing unconditional love goes a long way in modeling Christ before the workforce. It takes simplicity and godly behavior. That is "Work Is Worship" in a nutshell. We each have a ministry where we work. Therefore, "work is worship."

That whole scenario over the cup of coffee at MacDonald's that one day made me realize when we women fall into that trap of comparisons with each other that Satan is putting up a "smokescreen" and whispering lies right in our ears. We have to be in the Word every day, reading it, meditating on it, saying it out loud, so it registers in our hearts and brain and then memorizing it. That is how we hide God's Word in our hearts to protect us from wrong thinking that we are just not smart enough, attractive enough, cute enough, and talented enough as someone else we admire. We have to rely on the truth of God found in the Bible to lead us along the right path. God has a purpose for each one of us, but we have to show up!

Don't let the enemy cloud your thinking. I have to clean my eyeglasses daily to see clearly through them. Same with our hearts and mind. We must earnestly and passionately pour into scripture to cleanse our thoughts and keep them purified. God's truths must be implanted into our hearts and minds, so we don't forget them. We have to fight against the stronghold of insecurity and having a lack of contentment for who we are, and realize we have been created in Christ's image We are a daughter of the King, our Lord, and Savior Jesus Christ. So go—be His daughter and make Him proud!

⁑ Questions ⁑

1. We have been given numerous examples of people in scripture that have fallen flat on their faces. Name some that come to your mind. How did God overrule and show His power in the end?

2. When Jesus was tempted by Satan, He quoted Scripture. There is power in reciting out loud verses from the Bible. What verses can you find that give you God-confidence?

3. How does 1 Corinthians 10:12-13 help you be compassionate to others that have made mistakes too?

14
Worthy Of Praise

"You do your job, which is obedience. And God
will do His job, which is everything else!"

Mark Batterson

*"Finally brothers, whatever is true, whatever is honorable,
whatever is just, whatever is pure, whatever is lovely,
whatever is commendable, if there is anything worthy of
praise, think about these things."*

Philippians 4:8

What we think about determines what
we say. I have to ask myself and examine if I am dwelling and spending too
much time on frustrating and adverse circumstances, or do I think about joyful blessings that God has
already done for me throughout my day? My mind
keeps replaying and recalling upsetting situations.
Instead, I need to be watching in anticipation of
God working out everything for my good as Romans 8:28 says, rather than dwelling on the appar-

ent roadblocks or feeling hurt and mistreated. Oh, how I need this reminder!

Proverbs 4:23 warns us: *"Keep your heart with all vigilance, for from it flow the springs of life."* How that regularly takes diligent work. We need to set boundaries with our thought patterns and keep our focus on the sovereignty and power of God. We need to examine our thoughts and put up a HALT sign to our brain when we lapse into negative thoughts. The former popular business speaker, Zig Ziglar, called it "stinken thinken."

I want to reject negative thoughts. It takes discipline. I want to do better. I want God's approval of my actions. Paul gives six *thought patterns* that are required to be put into practice for us to acquire and maintain an active and healthy mental focus:

Think about these things:

- Whatever is true—God's Word is the truth. It rejects irrational thinking.

- Whatever is honorable—Personal moral integrity that is dignified and noble.

- Whatever is just—Doing the right thing. Reputable. Pursuing righteousness.

- Whatever is pure—All aspects of moral purity in thoughts and speech.

- Whatever is lovely—Pleasing, agreeable, pure, and beautiful in creation.

- Whatever is commendable—Admirable conduct, gracious—the best, not the worst.

Philippians 4:8 tells us that when we are filling our minds with things that will inspire our worship of God, rather than dwelling on our own shortcomings, then praise and thanksgiving will naturally flow. We must take action and destroy sinful thought patterns that are contrary to the truth found in Christ. Only then will we be praying without ceasing (1 Thessalonians 5:16-18). We must not stop.

The goal of obedience is found in Philippians 4:8-9. How can you be more obedient to God today than you were yesterday?

Individuals I disagree with, seeing them as being loved by God nonetheless, has spoken volumes to me. That is not my first normal reaction. I am trying to put this into my daily prayer time with God—asking God to help me see what is of "good report" with those that seem like sandpaper or are difficult personality types. It is helping me not to get as intimidated with those who are domineering, aggressive in intimidating, egotists know-it-alls, the underminer, superior acting, and prideful personality style types. I know my opinions are valuable too.

I receive Miriam Webster's Word of the Day sent to my email address every day. This week the word was *sacrosanct*. The definition said to be treated as if holy: immune from criticism or violation. Will I ever be immune from criticism? No, that would be unrealistic. But the lesson is that I must be entirely obedient to the Lord and want His acceptance above anyone else. He will then take care of the other details.

I discovered Proverbs 12:16 while reading a chapter a day in Proverbs recently, and this verse astounded me, which says, "The vexation of a fool is known at once, but the prudent ignores an insult." I wrote in my Bible next to this verse, "Really?" Then I took this a step further in studying 2 Corinthians 12:9,10, "But he said to me, "My grace is sufficient for you, for my power is made perfect in weakness." Therefore I will boast all the more gladly of my weaknesses, so that the power of Christ may rest upon me. For the sake of Christ, then, I am content with weaknesses, insults, hardships, persecutions, and calamities. For when I am weak, then I am strong." Paul is such a mentor to me in how he handled critics criticisms of him. He kept living for Christ and the spreading of the gospel always foremost in his life. Paul was a man of grit and grace. He had an unusual balance of proper humility and contentment despite hardships.

We must remember that God will be fighting our battles for us in ways we can't even imagine. I picture in my mind, God reminding me of this and winking at me and saying, "Linda—I got this!" That is a very reassuring picture.

God has placed you, and He has put me, where He has a divine purpose for us to flourish while we are on this earth. I am to show up because it is all part of His plan. It says in Psalm 147:11, "The LORD takes pleasure in those who fear Him, in those who hope in his steadfast love." God tells me He takes pleasure in me. Wow! I need to hold onto that when I feel intimidated and put down! When I feel like a failure and stupid, I need to read also in Psalm 149:4, "For the LORD *takes pleasure i*n his people; he adorns the humble with salvation."

So when I feel the darts flying at my back, I have to remember I am a child of the King. I am the daughter of the King. I am going where He wants me to go. I am writing what He wants me to write about. He is speaking to me through His Word when I read it. God cares about the birds in the air, so He cares much about me too. Here are some further promises to stand on and remember:

- God cares for me. 1 Peter 2:7, "Casting all your anxieties on Him, because he cares for you.

- God is working all things together for good and is the author of my story. Romans 8:28, "And we know that for those who love God all things work together for good, for those who are called according to His purpose."

- God will protect me. Psalm 46:1, "God is our refuge and strength, a very present help in trouble."

- God's purpose will be fulfilled no matter what. Psalm 138:8, "The LORD will fulfill his purpose for me; your steadfast love, O LORD, endures forever."

- God is rich in His grace and mercy for me. Hebrews 4:16, "Let us then approach God's throne of grace with confidence, so that we may receive mercy and find grace in our time of need."

- God's power is limitless. Ephesians 3:20, "Now unto Him that is able to do exceedingly abundantly above all that we ask or think according to the power that worketh in us."

- God is with me. Isaiah 41:10a, "Fear not, for I am with you; be not dismayed for I am your God."

- God loves me and knows my name (2 Corinthians 5:11; Isaiah 43:1).

- The Lord loves me, died for me, and rose again, that I may live for him (2 Corinthians 5:14,15)."

So dear sister, my lawn is not any greener. Your grass is not any greener than mine. Are you getting closer to eliminating the greener grass syndrome and quitting the habit of comparisons? I desire, as Paul did, to say at the end of my life, "I have fought the good fight. I have finished the race. I have kept the faith. Henceforth there is laid up for me the crown of righteousness which the Lord, the righteous judge, will award me on that Day, and not only to me but also to all who have loved his appearing (2 Timothy 4:7-8)." I am waiting to wear my crown of righteousness. Victory will be experienced at last, and I will not care whose grass is greener, yours or mine! I long to hear those apples of gold from my Savior—"Well done!" He won't say pretty good or very good. I want Him to say, "Well done (Matthew 25:21)!"

⸙ Questions ⸙

Our requirement is to follow Jesus; stay obedient, and rest secure in God's faithfulness. Your job is to obey, and He will guide and direct at the appropriate time.

1. Who do you know is a living example you would like to emulate in always thinking and saying right or noble thoughts? What verse will help direct you to obtain this achievement?

2. Who in the Bible is your mentor? Why?

3. What worship song has spoken to you of Christ's love for you and His amazing grace? Listen to it right now.

15

It Does Not Matter:
Clothed With Power From On High

It may take a lifetime for we women to stop feeling insecure, but let me share one point that God keeps reminding me over and over recently. Look at Genesis 1:27: "So God created man in his own image, in the image of God he created him; male and female he created them." Do you see that? He created male and female. We women were created in the image of God! Then in Genesis 1:31a, it declares, "And God saw everything that he had made, and behold, it was very good." Sister, God made you in His image, and He said when he was finished, "It was very good." God didn't say it was pretty good—no—"it was very good." The adjective good means—excellent, perfect, and terrific! That gives me great comfort. Doesn't it do that for you too? God made you in the image of God and made you excellent, perfect, and terrific!

God so loved me, God so loved you, that He gave His only begotten son, that whosoever believes in Him has everlasting, eternal life (John 3:16). That was one of the first verses I ever memorized as a child. I have paraphrased it just a bit, but the meaning is there to behold and grab! Jesus Christ died on the cross to save us from our sins and to give us eternal life if you accept Him, acknowledge that you believe in Him, and ask Jesus to forgive you of your sins and come into your life and take control, to become your Lord and Savior. God loves me warts and all. He loves you warts and all as well.

"God so loved the world" was a radical statement back in the book of John. Up until that time, the Old Testament and other Jewish writings had only spoken of God's love for Israel—for the Jews, God's chosen people. But John presented Jesus' death as the basis for salvation and the giver of eternal life to the whole world. When we believe that Jesus Christ came to die for our sin, and is God in the human flesh, and we genuinely receive the Savior, we are born into God's eternal kingdom. It is a supernatural work done by the Holy Spirit. That is when our faith starts. It is an ongoing process. As we read the Word of God, the Holy Spirit will point out to us what we need to grow in Him more fully. That is where we find guidance, comfort, a conviction of sin, hope, and sustenance for each day.

So if God loves me, knows my thoughts, knows my weaknesses, and helps conform me into His image, which is an ongoing process, then I do measure up to what He made me be because He was my creator and because He loves me. Let that sink in. Oh, I am a work in progress, and I mess up so many times and have to ask Jesus for forgiveness and thank Him for His generous mercy and grace (I am not giving myself any excuse). But we all are being conformed to Christ's image, being perfected, as James 1:4 declares, "And let steadfastness have its full effect, that you may be perfect and complete, lacking in nothing." The word steadfastness means to be resolutely or firmly unwavering in one's faith. Another figurative description indicates being watertight, as in the construction of a building or of a boat. Humbly remember, you have been clothed with power from on high and are being gradually transformed into Christlikeness through prayer and through reading the Word of God. Side note – God is more concerned about the decision-maker than the decision. We need to be fixed in our position in Christ and hold onto the fact that we are loved consistently by the Lord Jesus Christ.

I was shocked to learn while listening to an interview with Paul McCartney of the Beatles, recently on TV, that he suffers from fears. He admitted that he worries about being liked! He has worries and concerns in this area. Here this famous idol of music worries about people not liking him. How can that be after all of the gold records and awards he has been given during his lifetime? Everyone knows who Paul McCartney is, and people still listen to his music. Yet he too wonders if he is good enough or popular enough, and he must be a perfectionist and active people-pleaser. That has astounded me.

We must remember the simple song we all sang as children—"Jesus Loves Me!" That holds a wealth of theology and truth. Jesus loves you! If you are a Christian, you have part of the trinity living inside of you—the Holy Spirit. What really matters is that He has not rejected you. He is the great I AM. You are clothed with power from on high!

Yes, dear sister, approved and loved by God! Put your name in the blank from 1 Thessalonians 1:4 as Paul stated to the church in Thessalonica: "For we know, _____, loved by God, that he has chosen you, because our gospel came to you not only in word, but also in power and in the Holy Spirit, and with full conviction." Spend some time reflecting on what God is doing in you, with you, and around you.

⸱ Questions ⸱

1. What do you need to do to grow more in your relationship with God?

2. Layout all of your anxieties, insecurities, and inadequacies before God. Don't leave anything out. Now be still. Don't move. Be quiet. Sit in God's presence and wait for Him to speak to you. Write it down and dwell on that throughout the day, especially a verse that He brings to your mind.

3. What verses can protect you from the temptations of pride and also feelings of failure?

16
When Feeling Insignificant

"Are not five sparrows sold for two pennies? And not one of them is forgotten before God. Why, even the hair of your head are all numbered. Fear not; you are of more value than many sparrows."

Luke 12:6-7

I found a quote on Facebook one time that was a tweet from Timothy Keller, which said, "The greatest nightmare of the approval addict is rejection, of the power addict, suffering, and the control addict, uncertainty." Wow. That just about says it all. Of the three, I would no doubt fall into the approval addict category. I have a hard time dealing with feelings of rejection. Which one do you identify?

When struggling with feeling insignificant (we all have been there), think about Luke 12:6-7, "Are not five sparrows sold for two pennies? And not one of them is forgotten before God. Fear not; you are of more value than many sparrows." Sparrows are such small birds. They are not beautiful like an eagle, or a goldfinch, or even a woodpecker. Yet they serve God's purpose in playing an essential role in being insect controllers as they feed on all kinds of insects such as caterpillars, beetles, worms, and aphids. Sparrows are used in seed dispersion of grass, thistle, sunflowers, and weed seeds. By spreading seeds, sparrows help the survival of various plants. So my rose bushes need to have sparrows eating the aphids off of their leaves for their food! Luke tells us that we are of more value to our creator than many sparrows. God does not forget feeding the sparrows, and you, dear one, are of more importance than those tiny birds in your back yard, called sparrows.

Sparrows were found in high numbers in Palestine and were of very little value at the time when the book of Matthew and Luke was recorded. These birds were plentiful in population, troublesome, and five were bought for only about one hour's worth of wages in Jerusalem. Sparrows were used as food for the poor. Therefore Jesus used a striking example of God not forgetting one insignificant sparrow - and knowing the number of the hairs of your head show God's providential care over the smallest details of our life. That shows us we are of significant value to God. The minor aspects of our life are all noticed by Him.

Often we women struggle with our value or worth when we compare ourselves to other women.

Men do not seem to fall into this trap as often as us women (*as often* is the crucial two words). We frequently compare ourselves to a woman we think is better gifted and has more talents than we do, and it may turn into envy. Or maybe it is from someone that we feel is criticizing something we did from pure motives and intentions.

We differentiate other women's abilities as being better than our own, and we often feel we fall short and are not content. Then we struggle with needing approval and can't get away from the merry-go-round of feeling invisible and wonder if anyone remembers us or cares? It is a puddle (or lake?) of dissatisfaction—feeling insignificant. It is another fear we need to deal with that can turn into a stronghold.

We all judge people by their performance, their achievements, and how they look. We live in a very competitive culture. But God looks at the heart – not the outward appearance. Why is that not our first inclination?

Jesus declared in Luke 12:6-7, and in Matthew 10:31 that, He controls the timing and circumstances of all of His creation—even the sparrows and the number of hairs on our head. God commands it all.

As Matthew 10:31 declares, "Even the hairs of your head are numbered. Fear not, therefore, you are of more value than many sparrows."

It all goes back to redirecting our thoughts to God's truths and promises, and we must fight against the comparison idol. Here are some verses to keep close at hand when those thoughts of insignificance arise:

- Psalm 18:2: "The Lord is my rock and my fortress and my deliverer, my God, my rock, in whom I take refuge, my shield, and the horn of my salvation, in whom I take refuge.

- Isaiah 41:10: "Fear not for I am with you; be not dismayed,, for I am your God; I will strengthen you, I will help you, I will uphold you with my righteous right hand."

- Ephesians 1:11: "In him we have obtained an inheritance, having been predestined according to the purpose of him who works all things according to the counsel of his will."

- Matthew 6:26: "Look at the birds of the air; they neither sow nor reap, nore gather into barns, yet your heavenly Father feeds them. Are you not of more value than they?"

- Phillippians 4:19: "And my God will supply all your needs according to his riches in glory in Christ Jesus."

- Psalm 86:11: "Teach me your way, O LORD, that I may walk in your truth; unite my heart to fear your name."

"If you belong to Christ, God has a personal commitment to keeping you on His path – even if that means He will allow you to bang into a wall of dissatisfaction or get tangled in thorns of discontent every now and then ... When you find yourself walled off from where you want to be, don't focus on where you are. Rather focus on who God is and who He made you to be. Pray: Focus my heart on You, Lord, so I can honor Your name, not my wayward ways (Jennifer Rothschild, *Invisible: How You Feel Is Not Who You Are*)."

Are you still feeling not essential and that others do not notice you? Reboot your mind with Psalm 139:4-5, "Even before a word is on my tongue, behold O LORD, you know it altogether. You hem me in, behind and before, and lay your hand upon me." Then pray Psalm 139:23-24: "Search me, O God, and know my heart! Try me and know my thoughts! And see if there be any grievous way in me, and lead me in the way everlasting!" Amen!

Ask God to make you of benefit in your job, your family, and friends. You have an impact on those you encounter, and you have a more valuable role and are more beneficial than a few sparrows that are out your window eating insects. Every two to three people you encounter are in a crisis. God is preparing you for such a time as this to be of benefit in where He has placed you, to have the most significant impact and influence. You do not have to be a hero. You just have to be available.

·Questions·

1. Who can you encourage today?

2. How has God shown you He loves you and adores you?

3. Which one of God's attributes has He been using in your life recently? Grace, mercy, love, omni-present, or another one?

17

So What Is That To You?

I was stunned to read at the end of the gospel of John—Peter is asking Jesus how John would die? Jesus' reply took me by surprise as He said to Peter, "What is that to you? You follow me!" in John 21:22b and again in John 21:23b, "If it is my will that he remain until I come, what is that to you?" Jesus said that twice. Jesus repeated, "What is that to you?" in one sentence and then repeated it in the very next sentence. Jesus told Peter he shouldn't concern himself over that. Instead, Jesus told Peter to follow Him. He was telling Peter, "Don't worry about John, that is none of your concern. Your job is to follow Me!" He wanted Peter to realize Peter had to answer for Peter, and not for anyone else. We all want justice, don't we? Instead, we need to follow Jesus first and foremost. Oh, how I can identify and love Peter in the Bible. He might be my favorite disciple. I understand, Peter. Peter was emotional. He was passionate, and he was not lazy. But often his mouth got him into trouble (anyone else identifies with that too?), and he had regrets. Yet he was quick to ask Jesus for forgiveness.

I find it interesting that rumors spread even during the disciples' time between A.D. 70 and A.D. 100, which was the end of John's lifetime. How often don't we assume something from a conversation? Words are maybe inferred with meaning and not precisely stated, and we come out with the wrong sense and take for granted something that is not true. That sounds like something my husband would say to me. John 21:23a reports: "So the saying spread abroad among the brothers that this disciple (John) was not to die; yet Jesus did not say to him that he was not to die." What Jesus did say to Peter was, "If it is my will that he remain until I come, what is that to you?" That would solve a lot of jealousy, and feelings of injustice, if we recited Jesus' words to Peter and asked ourselves, "so what is that to you?" "Not any of my business or responsibility" is the right answer. God is in control. It is in His hands and His sovereign righteous plan.

We all tend to compare ourselves with other's lives, don't we? You are not alone. I do it too, which became the reason for me writing this book. It is a trap we often fall into—comparing ourselves to others and then finally realizing "your lawn (grass) is not any greener" than mine. Eliminating the greener grass trap and quitting the habit of comparisons can be done and must be done.

The next time you get your feet stuck in the sticky trap of envy, think of Jesus' conversation with Peter—"*What is that to you? Follow Me!*" This interaction happened after Jesus had appeared to seven disciples after His resurrection. Jesus was standing there in real life. Jesus reveals Himself again, after his resurrection, to the disciples by the Sea of Tiberias. The men had not caught any fish. This was the second instance where Jesus tells them to cast their net on the right side of the boat and assured them they would find some fish there. Jesus performs the miracle of the disciples hauling in 153 large fish this time. I find it interesting that this number of fish was recorded in our Bibles. Fisherman routinely counted the number of fish caught before selling them fresh at the market place. John, the author of this book, notes the nets did not break or become torn. The disciples knew it was Jesus in the flesh that caused this miracle to happen. John 21:14 states, "This was now the third time that Jesus was revealed to the disciples after he was raised from the dead."

There are numerous miracles that Jesus performed throughout His time on this earth. Yet, still, people did not believe in Him. The Bible tells us everything we need to know about the Lord Jesus Christ through whom we can receive eternal life. But alarming circumstances suddenly arise, and I doubt, lose hope, and am often like Peter. But I am quick to ask forgiveness of my Lord and Savior when I review verses that He has spoken to me.

When the Holy Spirit reminds me of God's truth found in His Word, and I then redirect my thoughts to God's truths and promises. Peter always seemed to lean to the extreme. He did everything passionately. He didn't do anything half-heartedly. No one else but Peter tried to walk on water to meet Jesus. Jesus told Peter his role was for him to "feed my lambs, tend my sheep, and feed my sheep." He was to disciple, mentor, and teach young Christian believers, help take care of their needs, and to instruct them and help them grow in their relationship to Christ (He was to be like a three-decker sandwich). Jesus told Peter, twice in this last chapter of John, to simply "follow me!"

So, I ask you, when you stumble and give in to worry, fear, guilt, doubt, and fuzzy thinking from comparing yourself with anyone else, repeat after me:

"So what is that to me? I will follow Jesus! Their lawn is not any greener. It is not my concern. Come, Lord Jesus! Fill my heart and mind with Your truth! Replace my insecurities with Your love, mercy, grace, peace, and hope in Your freedom, that is found only in following You."

Paul is a fantastic example of a man that lived by faith in God alone. He understood the right balance between Christian liberty and the grace of God. Paul preached it is how you live that matters in your character and what is in your heart, rather than merely what you eat or don't eat. Paul stated in Galatians 2:20-21, "I have been crucified with Christ. It is no longer I who live, but Christ who lives in me. And the life I now live in the flesh I live by faith in God, who loved me and gave himself for me. I do not nullify the grace of God, for if righteousness were through the law, then Christ died for no purpose."

Do you think during your day, very often, about the fact that Christ is living in you? Paul was saying that in his old life, he was self-centered, which was filled with envy, jealousy, and arguing. Paul was saying that it was in the past tense before his salvation. But in Christ, he now no longer lived for "I" and instead only lived to please Christ. Success was not his idol. He lived to serve and glorify God. Paul did not have a problem with EGO-Edging God Out, all because of the grace of God, shown upon his life.

I sometimes feel like my life is all being put into a blender. The good things, the wrong things, home life, family life, my work life, my writing, and God mixes it up altogether, due to His grace. Sometimes I feel, however, that this blender is overflowing. I then have to stop, pray for God to give me a blessing, and watch and wait in faith and trust in God. It doesn't necessarily happen in a few minutes. Still, moment by moment, I must depend on the Lord to work through me in making the best leadership decisions that can glorify God due to His grace and mercy bestowed upon my life, even (and especially) when I have blown it.

Paul lived strictly to please God and no longer lived for the applause of men because he lived by faith in God, who loved him and gave himself for Paul. Can you do that in getting rid of their grass is greener trap?

⁚ Questions ⁚

1. Whose are you, and what does then that mean in who you are?

2. How can you train your heart and mind to look for God to work in your life?

3. How can you stop being envious and live in a thankful spirit?

18

What Is Your Heart Set On?

"But sin, seizing an opportunity through the command-ment, produced in me all kinds of covetousness. For apart from the law, sin lies dead."

Romans 7:8

I was studying the book of Romans earlier this year. Romans is considered the Magna Carta of the gospel. Paul wrote Romans so that the Christians in Rome would comprehend how the gospel spoke to the issues that divided the Jews and Gentiles. Romans is full of teaching about the grace and goodness of God. It is where the peace of God is the result of understanding having the grace of God and recognizing Him blessing you daily.

There is nothing more profound in the Bible than in Romans 6. Paul says in verse one, "By no means! How can we who died to sin still live in it?" Yes, when Jesus died on the cross, our sins were nailed to that cross. The picture of baptism is being crucified with Christ and being dead to sin, buried with Christ (submersion underwater), and being raised to new life and having the power to live a new life in Christ. The old sin nature is paralyzed and deactivated, while other things are being made new for God's glory. This should be our battle plan every day, to walk in the newness of life (Rom. 6:4) that we have in Christ Jesus, one day at a time. That is the new identification you possess.

But read Romans 7:8. Paul states his vulnerability to the sin of covetousness. Paul, who was a saved Jew, who taught, preached, and wrote many books we read in the New Testament! He was raised in a conservative Jewish home. He worked amongst the people and helped change their lives due to the gospel. Paul was Christ's ambassador. Paul never lead anyone astray and was humble. Yet Paul says he struggled with coveting. In the NIV it states, "But sin, seizing the opportunity afforded by the commandment, produced in me every kind of covetous desire . . . (Rom. 7:8)."

Paul refers back to the Ten Commandments found in Exodus 20:17 and admits he recognized he had a struggle, a temptation, with coveting and revealed it to the church in Rome he hadn't met in person yet. Paul shows us he was human, saved by grace. Some commentators feel Paul was writing autobiographically about before his conversion experience. If that is true, then Paul is writing that he was indifferent to the demands of the law on the inner man. Paul was raised in a sheltered Jewish culture. He was taught the law from birth. But the fact remains that Paul points to himself as an example, be it pre-Christian or not, and explains the law of God is perfect, and as he grew in his understanding of Scripture, after his conversion, he realized how sinful he was.

So what does this word covet mean? It has to do with a strong desire to be consumed with the ambition for something one does not have. It is having one's heart set on something or someone. It usually is a desire wrongfully or without due regard for the rights of others. One example would never be having enough money and envying those that drive a Tesla or maybe a Bentley.

I wonder who or what it was that Paul struggled with not having contentment? Was it because he was so often in prison that he might have longed for a permanent home to feel safe in? Or did he think he couldn't talk or express his thoughts eloquently enough in comparison to some other teacher? We can only speculate. The Bible doesn't tell us precisely. Although it does say in 2 Corinthians 12:10 that Paul asked the Lord, three times to take some thorn in the flesh away, yet God told Paul, "My grace is sufficient for you."

So, what is the answer to stop the merry-go-round of:

- Not feeling as well-liked as you think others are.

- Not feeling as appreciated as others appear to be.

- Not thinking you are as popular as others might be.

- Not feeling you are enough or good at what someone else is in a position.

- Being discouraged by not receiving enough likes or shares on a Facebook post.

- I feel that others' dreams come true, and mine do not.

- I do not feel I can ever measure up or be good enough.

What did Paul do to combat these insecurities that come from comparing ourselves to others? I think Paul found it in the fact that God is the supreme judge. Paul recognized that some people are always down on themselves (1 Cor. 4), and Paul doesn't take much recognition of other's people's assessments or even his own assessment of himself. His mission and purpose was to please Christ and bring glory to Christ alone in pointing people to the gospel. We learn in Jeremiah 17:9 that the heart is deceitful and desperately wicked. Did you realize you need to guard your heart in the matter of insecurity and comparison to someone else? Going back to Paul, at that time, some people followed Apollos who was a polished orator. People were impressed with his speaking abilities and magnetic personality. Paul, however, was known as a great theologian. He had a highly trained mind that was sharper and keener than anyone else in comparison at that time. Both were significantly used by God. God made them both, yet they each had different gifts and talents in teaching and preaching and guiding the people regarding the Word of God. The only judgment that mattered to Paul was at the forthcoming bema seat of Christ, also known as the Judgment Seat of Christ (1 Corinthians 3:12-15). There is coming a day when the Bible says unbelievers will be judged in condemnation, while believers will be judged and given rewards (2 Corinthians 5:10).

Paul didn't live for the applause of people but for God's kingdom in mind. He was a leader and servant of Christ. Fix your leadership on being a servant of Christ and be content in where God has planted you and serve Him passionately.

Dear sister, take heart. Remember God's promise in Hebrews 13:5-6, "I will never leave you nor forsake you." Then write out on a card and carry this promise with you from Hebrews 6:10, "For God is not unjust so as to overlook your work, and the love that you have shown for his name in serving the saints, as you still do." Let that soak in deep! Claim the victory found in Jesus Christ. Christ will lift you to success in abiding in His love, care, and comfort. His grace is sufficient. It is enough. It fills up the hurt and replaces it with mercy and hope.

Dear friend, no one's lawn is greener than your own. Go fertilize and water your space by studying God's Word and making it your own Set your heart free from comparisons with others by holding God's promises tightly to you. Watch your grass grow and become a more vibrant green color as God fills up your heart with His almighty power of peace and lasting contentment. Now go—make him proud! You are a child of the king!

⸭ Questions ⸭

1. Are you one to be imitated? Or are you in a season of needing God to intervene and rescue you?

2. Who is it that you look up to and want to follow? Why?

3. What legacy are you leaving for your family? What will you be remembered for?

19

Look How Far You Now Have Come!

"For I am sure that neither death nor life, nor angels nor rules, nor things present nor things to come, nor powers, nor height nor depth, nor anything else in all creation, will be able to separate us from the love of God in Christ Jesus our Lord."

Romans 8:38-39

Nothing in the whole universe is beyond or outside of God's control. Romans 8:38-39 gives us hope and reassurance that any problem or situation does not confine God's power. Paul had experienced being in prison, persecution, famine, affliction on every level, danger, and the threat of martyrdom by the sword. He viewed it all with an eternal perspective (Rom. 8:28), because he was secure in Christ, despite all the evil around him. That was Paul's weapon against fear.

There is no circumstance God is not already aware of and didn't already know what was going to happen. He has a definite purpose for you as a single woman, wife, as a mother, as a woman in the business world, that no one else can do. You are it! God has given you talents and gifts to be of benefit. Your skills will glorify God right where He has placed you, as you use your God-given abilities to praise Him. Ask God to make you of benefit to your employer and to those you come into contact with daily and watch what a difference that makes!

When you are subjected to yet another trial, a problem that may at first seem overwhelming, you go through what I call several emotional stations:

- Rejection—You feel shocked. How could this happen to me? How could they treat me like this? You question if this is at all part of God's sovereign plan, and then you might feel guilt and shame for thinking those thoughts. I have.

- Enduring toleration—You ask God for a miraculous intervention. You wonder how long do I have to endure this? Despair may take up residence. You try and suck it up, and then you start to pray more.

- A light bulb turns on—As Jesus has been interceding for you all along, and as the Holy Spirit has been interceding for you according to the will of God (Rom.

8:26-27), you surrender and accept God's providential control, little by little—baby steps. Jesus is our advocate and defender. Remember, it is Satan, not God, that is the accuser.

• Fears dispelled by resting in God's love—We are freed from defeat due to the security of God's abiding love for us. Nothing can separate us from God's love, because of the way that Jesus, our heavenly Father, has lavishly poured His love within our hearts to the point of overflowing (Rom. 5:5). Our path had a detour. Affliction has changed us and was a vital addition to our story.

Don't we try to shelter our children in whatever way we can? There is this fine line in our responsibility of parenting in figuring out when to let our children learn from their mistakes and when to keep them from happening at all. I often wished I could prevent bad things from ever happening to our children. Warren Wiersbe in The Wiersbe Bible Commentary states:

"But God does not shelter us from the difficulties of life because we need them for our spiritual growth. In Romans 8:28, God assures us that the difficulties of life are working for us and not against us. God permits trials to come that we might use them for our good and His glory."

Have Romans 8:38-39 written down on a card or in a journal, and highlight them in your Bible. "For I am sure that neither death nor life, nor angels nor rulers, nor things present nor things to come, nor powers, nor height nor depth, nor anything else in all creation, will be able to separate us from the love of God in Christ Jesus our Lord." The next time you hit a roadblock, reach for Romans 8:38-39. Write down your problem and date it next to these verses. As you continue to pray every day, keep looking down at these words. Pray that the promises and the truth of Romans 8:38-39 will penetrate your mind and rule in your heart. Pray that the Holy Spirit will heal all your wounds and that He will teach you what God wants you to know. The book of Romans is a letter of comfort addressed just for you. Trust Him. Praise God for the profit that will come from enduring this hardship. When God does work out the answer, write it down, date it, so you can reflect back on it later and realize God has been glorified in you! Celebrate that! Look how far you now have come!

So my dear sister, lean into Jesus when you feel insecure and compare yourself to that other woman that seems all put together. When you think you are the second choice, when you feel less than perfect, when you feel inadequate, remember Moses, and Joshua, who both felt their speaking skills were not up to par. They were afraid the people would not listen to their leadership. They were men who had insecurities too.

Beth Moore had said during one of her teaching sessions that cashmere starts with a goat. Think about that. Cashmere sweaters are very expensive. A goat is a simple animal and look at what God created to come from a goat! Give up on being perfect. God can turn any detour into a Romans 8:28 lesson and reality. My grass is not any greener; your lawn is not any greener. It is time to eliminate the greener grass trap and quit the habit of comparisons. Worship God with the skills He has given only to you. Pray you will be of benefit right where He has placed you. Then watch how far you now have come. Hold your hand and arm raised high, with faith in God's almighty and sovereign plan, against all the odds. Guard your heart by staying in God's Word. Don't believe the lies our culture has fed us women in the media. Often pictures are edited and are not completely real. It is called marketing. Repeat Psalm 119:92-93, "If your law had not been my delight, I would have perished in my affliction. I will never forget your precepts, for by them you have given me life."

⁖ Questions ⁖

1. Do you see improvement in not giving into fears? Why or why not?

2. Did you have a closer relationship with your mother or your father? How did they affect your life as an adult?

3. What spiritual gifts has God given you? How can you use them to serve others better?

20

Transformer And Not A Conformer

"I appeal to you therefore, brothers, by the mercies of God, to present your bodies as a living sacrifice, holy and acceptable to God, which is your spiritual worship. Do not be conformed to this world, but be transformed by the renewal of your mind, that by testing you may discern what is the will of God, what is good and acceptable and perfect."

Romans 12:1-2

Romans 12:1-2 is the encapsulation of what it means to live in a way that pleases God. Here is the list:

- Embrace what God is doing and working in your life.

- Use discernment in not being merely a follower of our current culture without examining it against God's laws, for God's laws do not change.

- Let God change the way you think. Let His Word transform you into being progressively changed for His glory. Ask God to help you see things as He sees them.

- Renew your mind by feeding on His Word so you can determine what God's will is for you.

- Let the Holy Spirit be your counselor; give you courage, comfort, hope, and a positive perspective.

That is the abridged, condensed, and enclosed capsules of what it takes to please God. I love how The Message words Romans 12:1-2:

"So here's what I want you to do, God helping you: Take your everyday, ordinary life—your sleeping, eating, going-to-work, and walking-around life—and place it before God as an offering. Embracing what God does for you is the best thing you can do for him. Don't become so well-adjusted to your culture that you fit into it without even thinking. Instead, fix your attention on God. You'll be changed from the inside out. Readily recognize what he wants from you and quickly respond to it. Unlike the culture around you, always dragging you down to its level of immaturity, God brings the best out of you, develops well-formed maturity in you."

So, when you get up in the morning, before you leave your house for the day, plan time for just you and God to be alone together. No distractions. Turn off the TV. Open your Bible and read what God has just for you today. Follow some kind of plan. It might be reading through a book of the Bible—just a verse at a time or a chapter. Some like to read a chapter in Proverbs each day. Devotional books are extra. Spending time in the Word is what is of prime importance. Let it transform your heart and mind. Place what you have learned before God as an offering back up to Him. Ask the Holy Spirit to make it come alive and help you apply it to your life. Let God change the way you think until you know how God thinks, and you want what He wants and has purposed in your life. Don't let the current culture dictate how you feel. Develop discernment so you will be a transformer and not a conformer to society and where God has purposed you to live. Then God will bring out the best in you as you mature in your walk and relationship with the Lord. You will grow and develop righteous will power and won't power. Become strategic in how you direct your time and energy.

- Have you learned to long for God's approval alone? What gets in the way?

- How are you working on holiness in your life?

- Have you identified any idols that need to be abolished and confessed?

- Did you know nagging is a sign of bitterness and not forgiveness?

- Insecurity leads to idolatry.

Every day we have to choose to follow God's truths or give in to temptations of sin—anger, self-centeredness, pride, arrogance, envy, jealousy, grumbling, and not being content and thankful. Redirect your thoughts to the truths found in God's Word.

Surround yourself with people that bring out the best in you. Look to find someone that needs encouragement only you can give. Seek to serve others as God transforms your heart and mind.

Try to see the image of God in that person that criticized you. I know it is hard, but when you do that, think about how it changes your attitude. God is the creator of all human beings.

Does your happiness really depend on being liked by a person you have had a run-in with or let you down, or even hurt your feelings? What does your security lie in—is it a boss, a leader in ministry, a customer or client, a family member, your job, or is it in Christ alone? Are happiness and feeling sufficient idols you need to address in your life?

Are you making progress in stopping the comparison trap? Will you fall and regress? Yes, but you know how to pick yourself up again and march forth in the power and glory of God! Keep marching forward.

The grass is not any greener on the other side of the fence. God's purpose and will for your life is found solely in Jesus Christ. He promises abundant life, which is only found in Him. John 10:10 declares, "The thief comes only to steal and kill and destroy. I came that they may have life and have it abundantly." Put your name where it says "they"— "I came that _____ may have life and have it abundantly."

May your prayer be that you will be of benefit at your job, in your family, in ministry, wherever God places you. Paul's weapon was having a fear of the Lord rule his life. Paul experienced being in prison, persecution, famine, affliction, and the threat of martyrdom by the sword. Yet he wrote Romans 8:28 and lived it, because he was secure in Christ, despite all the evil around him. That was Paul's weapon against fear.

Pray that the Holy Spirit will heal all your wounds and that He will teach you what God wants you to know.

When you have relinquished being in the spotlight, embrace the freedom you now possess. Go ahead and breathe a sigh of relief. You have earned it!

The MSG version of Romans 12:3b says it eloquently: *"The only accurate way to understand ourselves is by what God is and by what he does for us, not by what we are and what we do for him."* Write on paper a list of everything that God is and what He does for you. I have a list started for you:

God is:

- Omnipresent
- Sovereign
- Omniscient
- Our great shepherd
- Defender, protector, shield, personal bodyguard
- The great I AM
- Jehovah Jireh-God will provide

What God does for me:

- Gives me God's sovereign grace and mercy
- Encompasses me with His love no matter how many times I fail Him
- Loves me unconditionally
- Guides me in His will as I read His Word, through circumstances, and wise counselors.
- Gives me courage.
- Works everything out for my good—Romans 8:28.

Now you add to this list in what God has done and is doing for you.

My word of the day, in my outlook this morning, was the word *sedulous*. The definition it said is:

involving or accomplishing with careful perseverance, diligent in application or pursuit. Be *sedulous* in your walk with God and fighting the comparison trap. May you go forth improving in not falling into the temptation to compare yourself with someone else negatively. It will take work. Bad habits are hard to break. Set out with careful perseverance, being diligent in your pursuit of accomplishing being content where God has purposed you to be, fulfilling His will for your purpose, which is not your position. Stand tall in your identity in Christ. Don't give up. Keep trusting God. Remember, Noah showed the world they were wrong when he finished the ark that God told him to build. Be sedulous.

You are a daughter loved by God! May the Holy Spirit pour His love into your heart to the point of overflowing (Romans 5:5). There is no grass greener on the other side of the fence. You are on a journey. Ask God to turn on His flashlight into your heart and mind so you can clearly know what He wants you to do. Dreams may change, and when they do, know that He has a better plan, He has a better purpose, and it is all for your good. Remember, you are blessed by God (Romans 4:7-8). Now go and walk in the fullness of God's light shining over you! Your grass is green, after all!

⁙ Questions ⁙

1. How have you begun to stop falling into the trap and habit of comparisons that feed on insecurities once and for all?

2. What blessings has God given you this week?

3. What verse popped out at you recently that clearly was God speaking to you—something special just for you?

21

Let It Go!

"Casting down imaginations, and every high thing that exalteth itself against the knowledge of God, and bringing into captivity every thought to the obedience of Christ."

2 Corinthians 10:5 KJV

Consider the thought regarding our female imaginations. They lie. I was involved in a very emotional situation in my job. I was impatient in something that was supposed to happen, and it was taking longer than it should have. So I was instructed to do something by my boss to fix it. It backfired on both of us. I should have prayed about it and asked God's counsel instead. I used human logic, and it made perfect sense at the time. But when the uproar occurred against what I had done, I felt remorse and a ton of guilt. Then my imagination went viral, and I felt like a total failure! I was afraid respect had been lost for me, and naturally, I hold that factor of my reputation with high regard. I moved into panic mode and earnestly asked God to fix it and to bring in Romans 8:28 into this situation.

Later that evening, I was sharing the morbid story with my husband and how I felt like a complete failure and was afraid my testimony had been lost. He immediately stated that my imagination was not valid. He even said we females let our imaginations run wild, and that was the problem. He comforted me in saying that I was not a failure and to stop it—stop thinking I was a loser because I wasn't, and then he started to list the excellent work ethic qualities I had earned and displayed in my sales job.

Paul told the Corinthians that their imaginations were a problem. Imaginations can be used for good in relation to creating art and being creative. However, our thoughts coming out of our brain in our minds can become distorted, and we are then actually engaged in a spiritual battle. Satan does all he can to rob us of joy and peace and tempts us with guilt, shame, frustration, and in the nasty net of feeling like we are a big failure—all from our imagination within our mind.

But if we remember to take every thought we have and commit it to God, He can do the proper cleansing and give us His truth to replace the enemy's lies. Which brings us to the question – who is in charge of our happiness—is it living totally for Christ, or the opinions of others? Our job is to live in obedience to Christ first and foremost. We are not going to get along with every single person, but as Paul said in Romans 12:18, we are to live peaceably with all men as much as we can – as much as we possibly can. It takes great humility, and frequently, we need just to let it go. Commit your anxiety to God—1 Peter 5:7: "Casting all your anxieties on Him, because He cares for you." So commit and hand it over to God. Let it go and ask God to make the results turn out for His glory and to make you be of benefit.

- Who can you bring out the best in today?

- How can you stop your imagination from lying to you as you reboot your mind with the Word of God?

- Who can you pray for today that has rubbed you the wrong way?

Each morning, get out a piece of paper and write on it "My Plans For Today. God, are they yours?" Remember, as you go about your day, you are in the presence of the almighty God. Colossians 1:27 declares, ". . . the riches of the glory of this mystery, which is Christ in you, the hope of glory." His presence assures us of our future life with Him when he returns. This is the competitive advantage you possess in your life. It is Christ in you, teaching you how to pray, transforming you as you read His Word (Romans 12:1-2), instructing you with the wisdom you ask Him for, and walking with you everywhere you go! That evening or the next morning, read over what you listed on "My Plans For Today. God, Are They Yours?" Notice if anything changed or something entirely new happened. Pause and reflect on what was essential and what wasn't. What happened in your expectations?

Today is a new day. Thank God for placing you right where He has placed you. No one else's grass is greener than yours. My benediction is from Paul, who wrote in Romans 15:13 NIV, "I pray that God, the source of hope, will fill you completely with joy and peace because you trust in him. Then you will overflow with confident hope through the power of the Holy Spirit."

Have you given your dreams to God? Have you asked God what goals He has for you in your work? Jesus brings rest and peace, and the devil brings restlessness, striving, and pain. Your identity is not in your success or failure; it is in Christ. I have to keep telling myself that over and over and over again. Our responsibility is to believe in the God who can, who is the great I AM. The Scriptures give us hope. Romans 15:4 states: ". . . that we through patience and comfort of the scriptures might have hope." Then Paul continues in saying in Romans 15:13: "May the God of hope fill you with all joy and peace in believing, so that by the power of the Holy Spirit you may abound in hope." That dear sister is where your joy resides. Be aware of simple needs all around you in being a light in the dark. You have Christ within you, and you are in the presence of almighty God! You have all you need as you are becoming complete in Him.

Satan reminds us of our failures, our mistakes, our regrets, night and day (Revelation 12:10) and Matthew 13:19 warns us, "When anyone hears the word of the kingdom and does not understand it, the evil one comes and snatches away what has been sown in his heart . . . " That is why we must keep our memory and our mind sharp by continually rebooting our thoughts with the truth found in God's Word. Scripture is fuel to redirect our thoughts to God's truths and promises.

I have a card on my desk, which I like to read throughout my day while working in my office: "Hold on to your Hope for He who promises is FAITHFUL." Hebrews 10:23. May you win the battle of feeling less when comparing yourself to someone else and being tempted to want to trade places with someone that appears to have a much easier life. May the God of hope fill you up with joy, fill you up with peace, and may you be filled with the life-giving energy of the Holy Spirit so that you will overflow with abounding hope, despite unfulfilled expectations. What other people have, or what other accomplishments other people have made is only looking at what you *don't* have. Start viewing what God *has* blessed you with instead of what you think is missing, and thank Him for His grace and mercy. He has a purpose in His divine vision, just for you, and has the long term plan. Repeat these words: "Your grass is not greener than mine and is not always greener on the other side!"

⸱ Questions ⸱

1. Write out a list of everything you are thankful for and review it regularly.

2. Who can you seek out to encourage today?

3. Who do you need to extend grace to today, just as God has extended His grace to you?

Conclusion

When you are battling the comparison trap, take your limitations in stride, and put your focus instead on knowing that God's grace is sufficient despite your weaknesses and gives you strength through the power of His Word.

Do not allow your burdens to make you harden up and lose your purpose in going forward. James 4:10 states, *"Humble yourselves before the Lord, and he will exalt you."* The NIV says, *"he will lift you up."* Every morning, lay it all out to God—all of your weaknesses, burdens, frustrations, etc. Seek His approval. Then lay down your will and be quiet before the Lord. You will receive God's sufficient grace and mercy for the day. The deepest struggles of our souls are just as great victories as any miracles found in the Bible. When we can control our temper, love others that have wronged us, having peace in the middle of a crisis, showing kindness without retaliation, having self-control with our mouth, all of these are just as great a victory as David slaying Goliath. This has been the lesson God is continually teaching me. God's sufficiency will bring me contentment, and that is how to eliminate the greener grass trap and quit the habit of comparisons that lead to insecurities once and for all.

One last important point to focus on in fighting against this trap of falling into the clutches of comparisons with others versus yourself. God will use everything, where you grew up, your upbringing, your talents, and your weaknesses so that you may serve Him in the future for His glory. God never wastes our time and always has a bigger purpose in mind if we commit our all to Him.

Look at Paul, Paul ministered in obscurity, as an unknown when he ministered in Tarsus for seven to ten years. He thought that was what God wanted him to do. But the LORD's plans were revealed to Paul when Barnabus sought to minister along with Paul, and take the gospel to the Gentiles, instead of only the Jews. This was the turning point in Paul's ministry, and the benefits of that ministry are still going on today.

Paul, who is such a mentor to me of a man that stayed the course and didn't give up despite his own weaknesses and mistakes, and his culture's controversial issues, had a past and present we get to learn from and glean the gospel truths he taught. Paul's history (his original name was Saul before his conversion) was his weakness and mistakes of witnessing and approving of Stephen's stoning. Saul-Paul had set out to destroy Christianity. But God had bigger plans for Paul and called him out that day in Damascus. This account is found in Acts 9. God used Paul to bring the gospel to both the Jew and the Gentiles. His education took place before his conversion, and he was trained as a Pharisee; therefore, he understood the Jew's thinking and culture. God used it all as Paul learned the tentmaking trade and served successfully as a missionary all for God's glory in taking the gospel to the Gentiles.

I think of my past. I grew up in northwest Iowa, in a small rural community. I was raised in a Christian home, and my dad was a teacher in the high school. He would tell my brother and me every night at bedtime when we were young children, make-up stories before going to sleep. He had a gift in teaching and making up entertaining childhood stories. In my senior year in high school, my English teacher, Mrs. Stracks, saw in me a gift at communicating through writing skills. She instructed me to be an avid reader, because the more you read, the better she believed would be your writing skills. I am thankful for her input in my education in writing as a senior in high school. Then I went to college to become a lower elementary teacher. I never became a teacher, but I still gained knowledge about teaching and use that today in my job as an outside sales representative that is now named as being an Account Manager. In writing my devotional blog and books, God is pulling my upbringing, my education, my sales job, all together. I have prayed and asked God to make me of benefit in my employment role of influence, and women's ministry at our church, and in the content of this book, all for His glory.

One of my closest friends, and a woman that I highly admire, said to me after I thought I had finished writing this book, that turned an inner light bulb on in my mind. Her statement and question to me was, "Think of things that God arranged when you were at a pause, due to the Coronavirus, shelter-in-home, shelter-at-place time." Her answer to me was this book that you are almost finished reading. That was a wow moment for both of us in God's plan and purpose for me while I was at a pause in life, in our shelter-in-place, COVID-19, pandemic situation.

Remember, are you seeking the approval of people or God? Be more concerned about being faithful, rather than popular. The Greek word for approved, tested, and acceptable is *docimos—dok'-ee-mos*. 2 Timothy 2:15 states, "Do your best to present yourself to God as one approved, a worker who has no need to be ashamed, rightly handling the word of truth." If we zealously pursue god's approval by aligning our heart with His Word of truth, God gives us complete acceptance, and His unconditional love for us never stops and never falls short. Then you will hear God's applause.

So when you feel lacking, give all of yourself to God and ask Him to use you for His glory and benefit. God wants to bless you. Some days you may feel like David before Goliath, rather than a Proverbs 31 woman. It is how our life becomes integrated with God establishing our steps (Proverbs 16:3) in achieving the Lord's purpose for us. Then wait and watch what God does as only God can do in your life as you eliminate the greener grass trap and quit the habit of comparisons.

Further Questions To Work On And Final Thoughts

1. Make a list of what you fear or are currently struggling with anxious thoughts. Look up the following verses: Psalm 3:3, Psalm 28:7, Psalm 84:11, and Ephesians 6:6. How do these verses apply to your feelings of insecurity? How does a shield protect from being physically harmed?

2. What does Proverbs 14:30 say that envy or jealousy will do to your body?

3. Emotions, good and bad, all flow out of the heart. Look up Proverbs 23:17. How can you replace the idol of envy and jealousy with "continuing in the fear of the LORD" all day long?

4. Why did the crowd choose Barabbas in Matthew 27:15-18? What lesson is to be learned by the Sanhedrin's jealousy, envy, and feeling threatened by Jesus' popularity in His authoritative ministry?

5. The heart is the center of our emotions, our mind, and our will. Read Mark 7:21-23. There are those words again—coveting, envy, pride. Jesus said they do what to a person? So how are you going to guard your heart to not allow those sins to corrupt and seduce you?

6. Read 1 Corinthians 13:2-4. What does love not do?

7. Put all envy away. Get rid of it. What does Peter teach the early church to do in 1 Peter 2:1?

8. Read Psalm 34 and let the words soak into your heart. What words speak out to you in this Psalm? The last verse of this Psalm gave me hope in one dark, and very anxiety-filled episode in my life many years ago: "The LORD redeems the life of his servants.; none of those who take refuge in him will be condemned." May you take refuge in our Lord today as you deny the stronghold of envy, jealousy, and comparing yourself to someone else and taking hold of the statement: *"Your grass is not any greener than mine!"* God is good. He is our help and shield.

9. Write your name in the blanks: 2 Thessalonians 1:11b-12: "May God make _____ worthy of his calling and

may fulfill every resolve for good and every work of faith by his power, so that the name of our Lord Jesus may be glorified in _____ and _____ in him, according to the grace of our God and the Lord Jesus Christ.

10. Remember God created you. Read Isaiah 29:16: "You turn things upside down! Shall the potter be regarded as the clay, that the thing made should say of its maker, "He did not make me"; or the thing formed say of him who formed it, "He has no understanding"?" What does this teach you about God? How does this change your view of you? What do you need to do in response?

11. How can you live out Psalm 16:8 today? "I have set the LORD always before me; because he is at my right hand. I shall not be shaken." Resolve to set your heart continually on heaven and be aware of God's presence with you and acknowledge He is right beside you. God's presence gives you value—not your work, not your boyfriend, not your husband, not your children, not your friends. All of that is just a bonus.

Live for Heaven—live for your eternal home. Reboot your mind with God's Word and towards receiving Heavenly rewards (Romans 14 and Corinthian Epistles). Everything else will not last. Success in business can be short-lived. There is always the question—OK, so what are you going to do for us tomorrow and next month? Ribbons for awards received in sports and even in AWANA are just that—awards for that moment's event.

When you look at someone else and envy their position, their gifts, and feel your shortcomings fall short and aren't enough, remember what you are seeing doesn't tell the whole story. Keep the big picture in mind. Guard your heart. Fill your mind with God's Word for it has the power to transform your life. Until you conquer this fear and stronghold of your grass not being as green as who you are idolizing, you will be a slave to wanting to be accepted by some inner circle, or as C.S. Lewis called it "the inner ring." Set yourself free from this bondage. You may not be wealthy, famous, or well-known, but you are the daughter of the king. Repeat the words in Psalm 19:14,

"Let the words of my mouth and the meditation of my heart be acceptable in your sight, O LORD, my rock and my redeemer." Seek out friends that share the same universal ethics and values as you do.

Take a Sabbath from insecurity and self-condemnation. 1 Corinthians 3:12 states that work that Christians do in Christ-like faith and obedience will survive and be rewarded up in Heaven.

Nothing will and can compare with that ultimate exhilarating and lasting joy! Live for that goal in mind. Then you can say: "I have eliminated the greener grass trap, and I am quitting the habit of comparisons once and for all!"

About The Author

Linda Killian was born and raised in North-west Iowa. She is the oldest of two children, and her brother still lives in Northwest Iowa. Linda now lives in Southern California. She and her husband have been married for forty-six years and have two grown children and five grand-children. Jonathan and his wife, Kim, have three children. Amy and her husband, David, have two children. Linda works full time as an outside sales representative for a chemical manufacturer and distributor in Los Angeles, California. Linda's formulations for her Supreme Anti-Wrinkle and Moisturizing Cream has received high reviews. Supporting and encouraging Christian women in business became a goal so she founded and is co-leader of Crossroads Community Church's Fel-lowship Of Women In The Workplace, ministry, located in Santa Clarita, California. Linda has one published Bible study book, "Taming The Lion's Roar. Handling Fear In The Midst Of A Trial, and a woman's devotional book, "Developing a Heaven-ly Mind Control. Devotional Thoughts to Reboot Our Minds With Truth. Linda writes a weekly devotional Blog for women called "Devotional Fuel to Reboot Your Mind—Redirecting Our Thoughts To God's Truths And Promises." She is passionate about studying God's Word, writing, reading, and encouraging other women.

www.ingramcontent.com/pod-product-compliance
Lightning Source LLC
LaVergne TN
LVHW011234080426
835509LV00005B/500